I0829511

LIGHTS
TOWARDS THE MIDDLE ROOM

Solange Sudarskis

11

Masonic wanderings

Copyright © 2024 Solange Sudarskis
All rights reserved.

CONTENTS

NB. To save the reader wishing to access documentation references on the web, links with simplified keyboard typing have been created with the *tinyurl.com software* .

1 THE GAME OF DEATH, THE DEATH OF THE I

Parricide, unlike fratricide, gives way to the disappearance of an overarching hierarchy. By killing Hiram, are the evil companions killing a brother, an authority or an under-representation of the divine?

Once the question has been asked, what should we do with our violence?

The basic problem to clarify is that we are all more or less violent. Yes, more or less, depending on the circumstances.

Obviously, we are all civilized and right-thinking and caring beings. The one and only weak point in all arguments is that no one is willing to admit their own violence. Our culture convinces us that this famous destructive energy is the result of frustration or external violence.

Psychoanalysis gives us a simple formula: the violence suffered induces aggression. However, Henri Laborit hypothesizes that the violence suffered by an individual is accompanied by biological disturbances which will, in response, modify their behavior until unleashed into violence.

Shouldn't she give him some excuses ? This very healthy message is paradoxically veiled by the moral messages of the epopty of the reception ceremony for the rank of master which refuse to recognize that violence is also inherent to life. Isn't the master presented as someone for whom virtues and loss of ego are more than strength or what "I missed"?[1]

Moreover, another simple equation tells us: "Without aggression, no life is possible. You have to kill to survive, to eat, etc. " ! We have known this for a long time, and we must realize that the simple fact of being born is a violent act for the mother and especially for the child. Is its primordial cry, in its passage from water to air, the fear of its announced death? Subsequently, will the recognition of his aggressiveness allow him to decide the questions of good or evil - and his guilt as a corollary - to tolerate tensions and to be able to "kill" this weight of himself? It is through cathartic play that he will recognize his pleasure in manipulating his aggression to dominate it, the psychologists tell us. " When we haven't played making accidents with little cars, or with figurines of firefighters who come to put out the fire by doing "pin-pon", we only know how to play in real life ," the child psychiatrist tells us. Maurice Berger.

Jacqueline de Romilly highlighted the psychological and social function of Greek tragedy which made it possible to externalize violence via a phenomenon of identification of the spectator with the actor-character and thus to evacuate it outside the walls of the city.

---

[1] Henri Laborit, *Inhibition of action* , video: <tinyurl.com/experience-sur-les-rats>.

The Masonic ritual accomplishes a fairly similar purification thanks to the visual spectacle it provides. The violence is theatrically staged, particularly during the psychodrama of the ceremony and the ritual of receiving the rank of Master. Does it not thus offer the framework and all the role-playing processes necessary for psychic development and its harmonization between darkness and light? In addition to the fatal outcome, we read in the *Ritual of the 3rd* ^{degree} *of the Marquis de Gages* : "bring me this unfortunate Companion to the foot of the throne of truth and justice by the march of the Masters... Then, we apply **a large blow with a roll** of cardboard or paper **on the left shoulder** of the recipient then they are made to leave the South with their left foot to go to the East from the North; he receives **a similar blow on the right shoulder** then he leaves from the North to go to the East, he receives a **similar blow on the head** in the East [2]. Nowadays, fortunately, the RER ritual is gentler, the test has become more allegorical: three rolls of paper or cardboard will be placed on the carpet in the West, South and North with which the candidate **will will be hit lightly on the back** , when he takes the three steps of Master, by the Brothers who will have received the order from the Venerable Master [3].

If the ceremony takes away his material plenitude from the murdered, it nevertheless opens the doors to the greatest of mysteries: the putting into perspective of life and death. Role-playing games make it clear, among other things, that there is work to be done on the fear in oneself of this absolute violence.

---

[2] See the engraving: <tinyurl.com/les-rouleaux-de-papier>.

[3] *Ritual of the rank of Master in the RER* , written at the Convent of 1782, completed by J.-B. Willermoz in 1802: <tinyurl.com/Rituel-maitre-RER>.

"The death of every man diminishes me, because I belong to the human race; so never ask for whom the bell tolls : it is for you that it tolls [4].

Isn't the Masonic work to learn to die by transmuting this fear of death into happiness of the present as a present of life?

---

[4]John Donne, *Devotions Upon Emergent Occasions Meditation XVII* . 1624. "therefore never send to know for whom the bell tolls; it tolls for thee", in the paragraph: *No man is an island* , ... (No man is an island): <tinyurl.com/pour-qui-sonne-le-glas>.

2 THE ACACIA WHO RUBS AGAINST IT LIVES THERE

The word "acacia" is said to come from a Greek etymology *a-kakos* (α-κακός) meaning "deprived of bad".

In all the ancient Mysteries, while the sacred plant was a symbol of initiation, initiation itself was the symbol of resurrection to a future life and of the immortality of the soul. With this in mind, Freemasonry substituted acacia for lotus, erica, ivy, mistletoe and myrtle.

The Egyptians had, in fact, chosen erica *or* heather as a sacred plant. In the mysteries of Osiris, a legend tells that Isis, in search of the body of her murdered husband, discovered it buried on the brow of a hill, near which an erica (heather), grew; after the recovery of the body and the resurrection of the god, when she established the Mysteries to commemorate her loss and healing, she is said to have adopted erica , as a sacred plant, in remembrance of the place where the *mutilated remains* of Osiris were hidden [5].

Among the Ancient Egyptians, acacia is present in funerary iconography; the acacia, *ished* , which means "that which gives happiness", was considered a sacred tree on the leaves of which Thoth and the goddess of writing were said to transcribe the names of the Pharaoh to wish him prosperity

---

[5] Albert G. Mackey, *The symbolism of Freemansonry* , Chap. XXVIII. *The sprig of acacia* : <tinyurl.com/brin-d-acacia>.

and long life ; its hieroglyphic name is *shen* (Chen is a ring which represents the concept of eternity, without beginning or end). In the granite sarcophagus of Amenophys II, an acacia branch was discovered on the body of the deceased.

The Egyptians used it to make papyrus secretaries, trunks and mummy chests. The *Book of the Dead papyrus of Ani* , discovered in Thebes in 1887 by Wallis Budge contains hymn and litany to Osiris. Section 5 of the litany includes a very special invocation: "Homage to you, oh lord of Acacia". This suggests that the Hiram of Masonic legend would be a symbolic avatar of Osiris?

According to Jewish tradition , the Hebrew term for acacia is "Shita" (shin-Teth-Hé, שִׁיטָה), but this word in gematria is worth 314, which is none other than the value of Shaddai, the divine name All Powerful. Thus through this traditional equivalence, the acacia branch, emblem and symbol of the master mason, takes us back through the veiled expression to one of the names of the GADL'U.

The Midrash relates that Jacob, through prophetic inspiration, saw that one day his descendants would come out of Egypt and build a sanctuary in the desert. Therefore, when he was forced to go down to Egypt because of the famine, he brought with him from Israel some shittim plants which he planted in Goshen. Thus, throughout the exile, the children of Israel maintained these trees which had become the symbol of their hope.

After having served as a pole for the traveling temple in the desert, the *shittim* were used to make the sacred furniture of the Temple of Solomon. The post, the pillar which marks the place, is said in Hebrew to be *amoud*. This word has the same root (aleph, mem, daleth, אמד , theosophical value 45) as the words *omed* (standing), Adam, *amida* (the heart of daily prayer) and *madoua* (Why?).

The term only appears once in the singular in the Bible in Isaiah 41,19 in a passage of a redemptive nature. "For I, Yahweh your God, take hold of your right hand and say to you: Do not be afraid, I am the one who helps you [...] I will plant the cedar, the acacia, the myrtle in the desert and the olive tree.

The etymological meaning of the word *shittah* means "the fire of hidden knowledge". Allegedly made of gold (it was only a project), internally protecting the ark, this gold would represent the beneficial forces brought into play to build the universe; the external gold, the opposing forces which are doomed to its downfall. The acacia itself was to be as protected as the Law preserved in the Ark, hence the two layers of gold. Acacia would then have the meaning of esoteric knowledge with its two golden facets. The acacia would therefore be the image of the free choice that we would make of knowledge and , in general, of the free will of man which must be protected.

The little-known acacia, (the acacia is known to me), that of the Bible, the Sittah or shittim (or sethim), does not correspond to any of the varieties present in France. It is a desert tree, with a twisted and gnarled trunk, made of very tight, extremely hard wood, the branches of which are covered with thorns measuring three to five centimeters long. It was with shittim wood that the Hebrews made certain parts of the sacred furniture including the tabernacle, the altar of sacrifices, the table of shewbread and the Ark of the Covenant.

The jagged appearance of the branches is not without problems for exegetes, some of whom think that there may have existed, in biblical times, an acacia of a more slender variety, with straight branches, while others refer to the legends reporting that the name shittim evokes cedars which would have been planted in the desert in preparation for the construction of the Ark by visionary ancestors [2].

In the Sinai, it is said that the acacia represents death because nothing grows nearby as its long roots (sometimes more than five meters) are hungry for the slightest trace of humidity. It is also said to be a symbol of immortality and purity, because it is reputed to be rot-proof.

In India and Africa , almost all ritual objects are made of acacia wood. Among the Bambaras of Africa, for example, a special ritual was done during the dry season, because that is when the acacia flowered again after losing its fruits and leaves during the winter; At home, old people at the end of their lives slept on an acacia bed, foreshadowing an eternal life in the other world.

Some Arabs dedicated a cult to the acacia until the day Kaleb received the order from Mohammed to destroy it [6].

The **Sanskrit term** for acacia is *saplaparna* which means "plant with seven leaves, seven leaflets".

Scholars _ call it *Cercis siliquastrum* . But, in tradition, there remains the Judean Tree, the tree celebrated in the Temple of Jerusalem. The Bible mentions acacia 29 times in the Old Testament. These occurrences are found mainly in the book of Exodus and relate essentially to the construction of the Ark (Ex 25.26.36) as well as that of the altar (Ex 27. Ex 38). In Israel, Bedouins recognize at least five species of acacia; some close to the mimosa of the four seasons of the Mediterranean, others to the winter acacia, less leafy and provided with simple or double thorns.

---

[6] Consult the article *L'acacia* by Henry Bac from page 72 of n° 2 in 1981 of the *Revue Initiation* : <tinyurl.com/L-Initiation-1981-2>.

The hollow thorns of this pioneer tree (one of the first to colonize open spaces) from **Latin America** , offer refuge and food to ants which, in return, protect the acacia from its predators and competitors. The relationship has become so close between the ant and the plant that it is symbiotic: the acacia is called myrmecophyte.

Acacias can form a community. When their leaves are attacked by kudus which come to graze on them, these trees emit a warning message which makes their leaves toxic. This message, in gaseous form (lethylene), is carried by the wind.

The builders of cathedrals , inspired by the symbols of the Shechinah, often carved the willow leaf on the pillars which represents immortality and divine light. In the ancient mysteries, this leaf was the golden branch , which becomes the acacia in Freemasonry carrying the meanings of innocence and purity. This presence of the acacia recalls the virtues of the founder Hiram, supposed to immortalize the one who is endowed with all merits.

It is with its branches that Christ's crown of thorns would have been woven. The *Precious Compendium of Adonhiramite Masonry* [7] explains that the acacia is there in memory of the cross of the Savior, itself made of this very common wood in Galilee.

In the traditions of sacralization of the acacia, it is found as a branch on the tomb of Hiram, crown of thorns of Christ, cross of Christ, coffin of Osiris, Ark of the Covenant of the Hebrews, Noah's ark, Tabernacle of Moses. Before Irenaeus, the ascia was an emblem imported by the Pythagoreans which they would have received from the Essenes [8].

---

[7] By Louis Guillemain de Saint-Victor, 1787.

[8] *New considerations on ascia* : <tinyurl.com/comprendre-l-ascia>.

Acacia is the analogue of the hawthorn, of the Egyptian and Christian Cross, of the Hebrew letter *Vav* , which means "link". It is the symbol of the link which unites the Visible to the Invisible, this life to the next; it is the guarantee of immortality.

René Guénon points out that many symbolic plants are thorny species such as the rose, the thistle, the acanthus. For him, thorns like points or horns evoke the idea of an elevation and can, in certain cases, be taken to represent rays of light. Note in the sense that Al Uzza means acacia, "thorn of Egypt" and that it is a solar symbol.

The importance of the symbol of the acacia in the 3rd ^{degree} allowed William Hutchinson (1732-1814), member of the *Royal Society of Antiquaries,* to nickname the Freemasons **the** *Acacians* .

Note that in an allegorical painting from 1753 entitled *The mysteries shown here are those that only one mason can know* , King Solomon draws the Pythagorean theorem, he looks towards two characters sitting in the sky on clouds. One of them is undoubtedly Time Chronos who holds the death scythe in his right hand with an ouroboros and an acacia branch in his left hand.

Masonic acacia might not be a tree as shown above. This could be ascia deformity. There are two *asciae* . One, an adze opposite a hammer, was used for working wood and stone. The other, a hoe opposite a two-sided rake, to stir the earth. The funerary ascia, not carrying the bifid rake, would therefore be the hammer adze. It would have been used to cut funerary steles. The verb *deasciare* obviously qualifies the opposite act of *asciare* , the second, symbolic meaning of which could be "to seal a tomb under the ascia to give it an inviolable character". The primary meaning would be: **to dedicate the tomb** by flattening the funerary block with the ascia. *Deasciare* would then be: **destroy this dedication** by hammering the stele. So the distorted word **acacia would be a tool** with a symbolic dimension, swapped in Prichard's *Manuscript Masonery Dissected* (1730) by "cassia".

3 TUBALCAIN, A SULPHUROUS CHARACTER?

Tubalcain, like Hiram, is only a secondary character in the biblical text.
He is part of the lineage of the Cainites and only appears with his siblings, both in the Bible where his name appears only once, and in the texts of the *Old Charges* .

So what is its interest in Freemasonry?

The root of the name Tubalcain would be in Hebrew thu, bal, cain, the one who breathes fire, a name taken up in Latin by Vulcanus. Melting the metal and reforming it corresponds to the " *solve et coagula* " of hermetic alchemy.
It is Gérard de Nerval who romanticizes his relationship with Adoniram, which justifies, although used as a password of the 2nd degree in Anglo-Saxon rites, to evoke his legend in the 3rd degree.

I – The character

According to the Bible (Genesis IV, 22), Tubalcain made all kinds of instruments of copper and iron. He is presented as the son of Lamek and his second wife Çilla, therefore he is the grandson of Cain, born around the year 2975 BC. AD Enoch became father of Irad; this one begat Mehouyaél, who begat Lamech. Lamech took two wives, the first named Ada, and the second Cilla. Adah gave birth to Jabal, the descendant of those who dwell in tents and lead flocks. His brother's name was Jabal: he was the stock of those who wield the harp and the lyre. Cilla, for her part, gave birth to Tubalcain, who made all kinds of instruments of copper and iron, and who had Naama as a sister.

The name comes from the union of that of Tubal with Cain. Tubal (8 times: Gen 10.2; Is 66.19; Ez 27.13; 32.26; 38.2.3; 39.1; 1 Ch 1.5) would be a people and/or a country of Asia Minor (People of Asia Minor, probably Phrygia and Cilicia, or peoples of the shores of the Black Sea.), always associated with Meshek. Meshek and Tubal are two of the seven sons of Japheth according to Gen 10,2 // 1 Ch 1,5.
As for the name Cain, there are two possible etymologies. The Hebrew word qayin can mean "smith" or, using the root qnh "I have acquired" (cf. Gen 4: 1).
.

It is believed that it was from Tubal-Cain that the pagan Romans took the idea of their Vulcan; the root of the name Tubalcain would be in Hebrew thu, bal, cain, the one who breathes fire, a name taken up in Latin by Vulcanus. The ending of the name and the work to which Tubal-Caïn devoted himself make this conjecture quite probable. Likewise, he corresponds to Hephaestus, among the Greeks: Greek god of fire and forging; to Vulcan among the Romans, to Tvashtri in India, to Ptah in Egypt, to the Great Yu in China, to Ogun among the Youbas of Africa, to Brahmanaspati in India. It is also Gobban Saer, the Janus of the Celts, who represents the union between technique and art, Gobban the blacksmith, and Saer, the builder, skilled in all the Arts, who can be identified with the figure of Hiram .

The fire of all these legendary blacksmiths is a creative fire, it illuminates and does not burn. It cannot be dissociated from the Light without which nothing would be, because it establishes the forms of the apparent world.

It is in *the History of the Queen of the Morning and Soliman, Prince of Geniuses by Gérard de Nerval* in chapter VII, *The Underworld* [9]that we find the romantic meeting of Hiram and Tubalcain. The basis of this legend is , however, different from the Masonic legend: it is stated that Adoniram is in reality a descendant of Cain through his father Enoch; her Promethean ancestry is revealed to her as well as the curse that weighs on her.

In summary: Dragged as in a dream into the depths of the Earth, Hiram learns from the very mouth of Tubal-Caïn the essentials of the tradition of the Cainites, these blacksmiths masters of fire. Tubal-Caïn, in the heart of the Earth, then shows Hiram the long succession of his fathers: Enoch, who taught men to build buildings, to group themselves in society, to cut stone; Hirad, who once knew how to imprison fountains and direct fertile waters; Maviël, who taught the art of working cedar and all woods; Mathusaël, who imagined the characters of writing; Jabel, who pitched the first of the tents and taught the men to sew camel skins; Jubal, who first stretched the strings of the cinor and the harp, and knew how to draw harmonious sounds from them; finally, Tubal-Cain himself, who taught men the arts of peace and war, the science of reducing metals, of hammering brass, of lighting the forges and of blowing the furnaces. Cain then himself teaches Hiram how, over the ages, the children born from him, son of the Elohim, will constantly work to improve the lot of men pursued by an unjust god who favored Abel.

---

[9] *History of the Queen of the Morning and Soliman, Prince of Geniuses by Gérard de Nerval* in chapter VII, *The Underground World*, 1851: <tinyurl.com/le-monde-souterrain>.

II – Tubalcain and the *Old Charges*

In Masonic tradition, the earliest reference to Tubalcain dates back to the *Cooke Manuscript* around the year 1400.

We learn that the children of Lamech, among whom Tubalcain, would have engraved on 2 columns (while according to the historian Josephus, it would have been Seth), one of marble to resist water, the other of brick to resist the fire, all of their scientific and artistic knowledge so that they survive the flood, thus symbolizing the transmission of Tradition.

This is what the *Cooke Manuscript* says

" Adam's direct descendants during the 7th Adamic age before the flood included a man named Lamech, who had two wives, one named Adah and the other Sella. By his first wife Ada he had two sons, one called Jabel (Yabal) and the other Jubal (Yubal).

The elder Jabel was the first to invent geometry and masonry. And he built houses and his name is found in the Bible: he is called the father of those who dwell in tents, that is, dwelling houses.

He was Cain's master mason and leader of all his works when he built the city of Enoch, which was the first city ever built. And it was built by Cain son of Adam, and he gave it to his own son Enoch and named the city after his son and called it Enoch, but now it is called Effraym.

It was there that for the first time the science of geometry and masonry was practiced and developed as a science and art. We can also say that it was the basis and foundation of all science and technology. and this man Jabel was also called Pater Pastorum.

The Master of Stories as well as Bede, the De Imagine Mundi, the Polychronicon and many others say that he was the first to divide the land so that every man could know what his personal land was and work on it as for his own good. . In addition, he divided the flocks of sheep so that everyone knew which sheep they had, so we can say that he was the inventor of this science.

And his brother Jubal or Tubal, was the inventor of music and song as Pictagoras says according to the Polychronicon, Isidore says the same in his Etymologies in the 6th book: he notes there that he was the inventor of music, singing, the organ and the trumpet and that he invented this science by listening to the rhythm of the hammers of his brother, who was Tubal-Caïn.

Just as the Bible, in its 4th chapter of Genesis, says that Lamech had from his other wife, who was called Sella, a son and a daughter whose names were Tubal-Cain for the son and Naama for the daughter. Some say, according to the Polychronicon, that she was the wife of Noah but we cannot confirm this.

You should know that his son Tubal-Cain was the inventor of the art of blacksmithing and other arts of metals, that is to say, iron, steel, gold and silver according to some doctors. As for her sister Naama, she invented weaving, because previously we did not weave but we spun and knitted fabrics and we made the clothes we could. Naama invented the art of weaving and that is why it was called women's art.

Now these three brothers and sister learned that God wanted to take revenge on sin by fire or by water and they tried to save the sciences that they had invented. They thought, and said to themselves that there were two kinds of stone, one of which resists fire &endash; this stone is called marble &endash; and the other floats on water – and it is called lacerus.

So they imagined writing all the sciences they had invented on these two stones ; in case God took revenge by fire the marble would not burn and if he chose water, the other stone would not sink.

They asked their elder brother Jabel to make two pillars of these two stones, namely marble and lacerus, and to inscribe on these two pillars all the sciences and techniques that they had invented. He did so and completed everything before the Flood.

Although they knew that God was going to send his vengeance, they did not know whether it would be by fire or by water. By a sort of prophecy they knew that God was going to send one to the other. So they wrote their sciences on the two stone pillars. Some say that they carved the seven sciences on the stones , knowing that punishment would come.

In fact God sent his vengeance so that such a flood occurred and the whole earth was drowned. And all men on earth perished except eight: Noah and his wife, his three sons and their wives. From these three sons descends all humanity. Their names were Shem, Ham and Japheth. This flood was called Noah's Flood because he and his children escaped.

And many years after this flood, the two pillars were found and, according to the Polychronicon, a great cleric, named Pictagoras found one and Hermes, the philosopher, found the other. And they began to teach the sciences which they found written therein ."

III – Tubalcain and Freemasonry

Note that in the *Constitutions known as Anderson* , the engraving of the columns is attributed to Enoch [10]: "for, by some vestiges of Antiquity, we know that one of them, the pious Enoch (who did not die but was transported alive to Heaven), prophesied the final conflagration on the Day of Judgment (as SAINT-JUDE tells us) and also the general flood for the punishment of the World. This is why he raised two large pillars (others attribute them to Seth), one of stones and the other of bricks on which the liberal sciences, etc., were engraved. And that the stone pillar remained in Syria until the days of Emperor Vespasian.

Its evocation in rituals

In the Rectified Scottish Rite, **this was the apprentice's initial password** . At the request of Jean-Baptiste Willermoz, who would have been inspired by Countess Marie-Louise de Monspey, known as Églé de la Vallière (the Unknown Agent), **canoness** of Remiremont, a psychographic medium, this word was replaced in 1785 by Phaleg . For Willermoz, it was a contradiction to give the apprentice this rallying word after having made him abandon all the metals which are the emblems of vices. He considered that "the descendant of Cain was also the father of all abominations, an unworthy being guilty of the most shameful prevarications in the carnal way, that he had only discovered the way of forging metal by diabolical and profane operations, that he could have stopped the course of these evils, but driven by his own lust, he avoided the

---

[10] *THE CONSTITUTION, History, Laws, Charges, Orders, Regulations, and Uses, OF THE Most Worshipful FRATERNITY of Accepted Free Masons; according to their general ARCHIVES, and their Faithful TRADITIONS of many Centuries, p.1 : <tinyurl.com/Constitution-Anderson>.*

bad angels in women [11]. Yes, it was a nun who "moralized" the Masonic RER password!

"Tubalcain was therefore rejected from the rituals in favor of Phaleg by the Provincial Directory of Auvergne for the following reasons: " Tubalcain is the son of Lamech, a bigamist. Inventor of the art of working metals, he cannot be attributed to the Apprentices who have just abandoned them. He is the emblem of vices, particularly sexual. Representing an antediluvian lineage erased by God, he must give way to Phaleg, founder of the only true initiation . This modification, made on May 5, 1785 by a decision of the Scottish Regency, was poorly accepted by many brothers belonging to this Rite.

In the Emulation Rite, Tubalcain is the **passage word giving access from the 2nd** [to] **the** [3rd] **grade** .

At the York Rite, Tubalcain is the **name of the claw** of passage from companion to master, serving as a password to the 2nd [degree], as appears in the exchange between the 1st [supervisor] and the 1st [expert] in the instructions of the degree: "-Does she have a name? -Yes — Will you give it to me? — This is not how I received it and I will never communicate it like this . — How do you dispose of it? — By spelling it out or by syllable. — Give it by syllable and begin. — Start yourself. — It's up to you to start ." . The word Tubalcain is given by syllable between the first expert and the Venerable Master Then completely by the 1st [expert] . This claw is one step below the true claw of the master.

At REAA, this is the **Master's password** . "This word is TULBAKAIN, which we have adopted because of the intimacy which must exist between us and the first Vulcan in the universe. We call this a waking word, because we

---

[11] **A mystic from Lyon and the secrets of Freemasonry Jean-Baptiste Willermoz by Alice Joly: <tinyurl.com/Tubacain-et-Willermoz>.**

require it to be spoken before what was once known, namely JAKIN [12].

IV – Interpretation

For Irène Mainguy, because it includes the names of Abel and Cain in its name, Tubalcain "brings together in itself the complementary qualities of a fratricidal antagonism by reintegrating the central point of Primordial Unity" [13].

For Hervé Tremblay, the genealogies of the first eleven chapters of Genesis are intended to describe peoples (Gen 5) and justify the appearance of different aspects of human life, such as arts and crafts. In Gen 4:20-22, the three castes of cattle breeders, musicians and traveling blacksmiths are linked to three ancestors whose names resonate and recall the professions of their descendants: Yabal (ybl "to drive"); Yubal (yôbel "trumpet"); Tubal (name of a people from the north, in the land of metals). Tubal-Cain is said to be "the ancestor of all copper and iron smiths ". This means that genealogies are not very reliable historically and that names are rather creations intended to account for the world as it is.
Tubalcain, the blacksmith, works metals and is spiritually a continuation of the Cainite lineage. The blacksmith is one of the builders and learns to be through creation. He has the knowledge of the four elements : the metal is extracted from the earth, it is transfigured by fire, itself fanned by the air then tempered by water in order to become a useful

---

[12] Solomon in All His Glory or the Master-mason, translation of Unmasked Freemason or the True Secret of the Frans Masons of 1751: <tinyurl.com/Salomon-dans-toute-sa-gloire>.

[13] Fabien Bertand, *Crossed perspectives on Freemasonry* , from p. 169: <theses.fr/2009BOR21677>.

instrument for plowmen or warriors. He forges swords, an initiate's work because they are sometimes endowed with magical power, which requires knowing and mastering the forces contained in these elements. The blacksmith masters fire and thanks to it transforms the metals that come from the depths of the earth. His power is ambivalent, he can be as evil as beneficial because he forges weapons to wage war and like Tubalcain who, according to the testimony of Philo and the apocryphal book of Enoch, cited by Tertullian, also used in his works the gold, silver, etc., of which they then made idols to worship them.

Changing Cain's password to Phaleg amounts more philosophically to substituting the forge for the benefit of the dispersion of the Word. This point is far from being anecdotal in a Masonic practice which will reintegrate the dimensions and forms of this same Word by making it flesh in the spirit of the Gospel of Saint John. The choice is clear and the determinism deliberately Christian which disperses the forge of Cain for the benefit of the lost Word. It is no longer a question of a multidisciplinary construction, of a polytechnic architect, but of the capstone which had been rejected [14].

The work of the forge means the constitution of being from non-being. The forge is the allegory of the heart and the bellows represent the lungs.

Melting metal and reforming it corresponds to the *burst and coagula* of hermetic alchemy, creative work par excellence, because to create is to recreate.

On another level, according to Guy Barthélémy, the political meaning of Nerval's fable is clear: those who produce the

---

[14] < tinyurl.com/Phaleg-et-Willermoz > .

riches of the earth, but who also allowed men to escape from their animality, because among these banished people, there are the one who invented the city, the one who invented weaving, the one who designed the first musical instrument who are unjustly oppressed by this God who wants to abusively keep men in a state of ignorance and by those who serve as his relay : the kings, these despotic ministers of Adonai. Knowledge and freedom can therefore only flourish in a socialist struggle which shifts towards calling into question the one God.

Lights towards the Middle Chamber

4 THE LEGENDS OF NOAH

Noah, a savior angel of the flesh in some way!

The Book of Enoch records that Lamech's wife gave birth to a child "whiter than snow, redder than a rose; his hair is whiter than wool, and his eyes shine like the sun ; when he opens them, he fills the house with light. And immediately after he came out of the hands of the midwife, he opened his mouth and blessed the Lord." Lamek was terrified by the miracle and went to see his father Metoushelah to tell him that he had fathered a child different from all the others, who consulted Enoch. Enoch explained that because of the evil of the world, a flood was to come, but that Noah and his children would be spared [15].

Noah (Noa'h) would have lived 950 years, having had three sons: Shem , Ham and Japheth. His story is told in the Bible (Genesis 6 to 9). Noa'h presents himself as a mirror of Bereishit. With the flood, God destroys the world he created and the construction of a new humanity is now in the hands of Noah and his children. A second creation which involves a new structuring of the family with its conflicts, its impasses and its blessings [16].

---

[15]Chapter 105: <tinyurl.com/Book-of-Enoch>.
[16] Rony Klein, Akadem: <tinyurl.com/un-deuxieme-commencement >.

Like the Sumerian heroes whose names were Ziusudra (Prolonged Life), Atrahasis (Very Wise) or Utnapistim (He who found life), before the flood, Noah gathered what was scattered in the ark (teva, תבה), floating crate to save the living from the creation of the predicted flood. He would perhaps also have carried written or symbolic knowledge ensuring the essential transmission of knowledge that was as spiritual, cultural as technical and scientific, a summary of the main knowledge of his time.

The water ordeal.

There is danger of death in the ordeal, and it is a danger for the rest of humanity and the rest of creation, but one over which the inhabitants of the ark will triumph. The test is overcome because of the good faith of Noah, a righteous man who walked with God (who follows his law). The episode of the flood allows us to move from the First Age of the world to the Second, which represents both a new birth for humanity and creation, and a new alliance between God and man.

It is noteworthy that the empire builders are born in a basket floating on the waters (Osiris in a basket-chest on the Nile, Sargon founder of the empire of Akkad on the Euphrates, Moses on the sea of reeds, Romulus and Remus on the Tiber). The sarcophagus is at the same time a basket full of life like Noah's ark .

The Jesuit Philippe Labbé, towards the end of the 17th [century] , [17]uses Noah's flood as a hinge between the 1st and 2nd era of the History of the world as St Augustine had done before

---

[17]and profane history with the observations necessary for the study of Chronology, Paris, 1666: <tinyurl.com/Abrege-Histoire>.

him in 426 in *The City of God* (Book XV concerns the "first age" of humanity up to Noah, Book XVI concerns the "childhood", which corresponds to the biblical episodes from Noah to Abraham).

Other legends relate stories of the flood [18].

A legend is present **among the Greeks** . Filled with anger at human perversity, Zeus chose the flood to wash the face of the earth. Poseidon summons the rivers to overwhelm the cities and whoever is not submerged dies of hunger. Only Mount Parnassus rises above the water. Deucalion, son of Prometheus, and Pyrrha, his wife, took refuge in a small boat. When Zeus sees that these survivors are honest and pious, he disperses the clouds. The waters flow back and the sea returns to its ancient shores. Arriving at Mount Parnassus, Deucalion and Pyrrha thank the gods, and see only a desert around them. Imploring Zeus to help them restore life to the earth, they are advised to veil their heads and throw their grandmother's bones behind them. Deucalion understands that this grandmother is Earth. Helped by Pyrrha, he picks up stones which he throws over his shoulder. The stones that Deucalion throws are transformed into men. Those thrown away by Pyrrha turn into women.

A similar myth is known **in India** , which was once partially under Greek cultural influence. The myth of the Flood first appears in the Satapatha Brahmana, a ritual probably dated to the 7th century BCE. Here, it is a fish gifted with speech which warns Manu of the imminence of the Flood. He firmly advises her to build a boat. When disaster strikes, it is this fish that pulls the boat towards the north and stops it

---

[18] *The myths of Noah's ark* : <tinyurl.com/mythes-arche-de-Noe>.

near a mountain. Manu patiently waits for the waters to ebb. Then he offers a sacrifice and obtains a daughter from the gods. He unites with her, engendering the entire human race. In the Mahabharata, Manu is an ascetic. In the Bhagavata Purana, it is the ascetic king Satyavrata who is warned of the approach of the Flood by Hari (Vishnu) who took the form of a fish. But, in Hindu myth, nothing seems to connect the flood with any resentment of the Gods towards men.

The episode of Noah's drunkenness and nudity (Genesis, 9, 18 to 27) gave rise to numerous comments including those of the idea of a castration of the patriarch by Ham (or his son) at the like the Egyptian Osiris, the Hittite god Anu or the Greek Cronos [19]. It is therefore surprising that eunuchs were banned in Freemasonry [20].

In Hebrew yayin (יין), "wine" has the value 70 like the word sod (ס ו ד), the secret. With Noah's drunkenness, should we not understand that it is a secret that is hypostatized? Drunkenness must then be interpreted as a mystical ecstasy, a knowledge of a higher rank which must be veiled or protected in an ark (téba). In this second interpretation, Noah's nudity is not his sex, but the symbol of a revelation which makes him a true initiate. Would Japheth who turns away refuse to approach the mysteries, perhaps being too young [21]?

Graham Manuscript dating from 1726 was discovered which is believed to be a copy of an older document reporting this

---

[19] Robert Graves and Raphaël Patai, *The Hebrew Myths* , Fayard, 1963, p.129 to 134.

[20] Hartmann Schedel, *Liber chronicarum* , 1490, p.100: <tinyurl.com/Liber-chronicarum>.

[21] *The Furtmeyr Bible,* p.15: <tinyurl.com/bible-de-Furtmeyr>.

legend of Noah which does not appear in the Bible. Shem , Ham, and Japheth approached the tomb of their father Noah, hoping to discover the secret saved from the waters that he would have held. They agreed to adopt as a secret, if they did not find the real secret, the first thing that came under their notice. They only found a corpse in the process of decomposition, they pulled out a finger which detached itself, then the wrist, then the elbow: they raised the dead body and supported it by placing foot against foot, knee against knee, chest to chest and cheek to cheek. Then not knowing what to do, they put the corpse down and one said "there is marrow in this bone", the second said "the bone is dried up", the third said "it stinks". They pronounced the name considered today as a substitute word. The translation of *marrow in the bone,* "the marrow in the bone" would be one of the origins of the substituted word and can be explained symbolically by "the sap which is in the tree", the light is interior and it transcends the apparent form of death.

One of the reasons which made Noah abandon Noah in favor of Hiram, although almost unknown in the Bible, is undoubtedly that the heroic act of Hiram, who prefers death rather than revealing secrets, is more prestigious, or all at least more effective than the case of Noah who died of old age.

Lights towards the Middle Chamber

5 THE LEGENDS OF HIRAM

The origins of legends

The legends of the stone are numerous. Blood (animal or human) must be shed to ensure the construction of the building . John SM Ward in his book *Who was Hiram Abiff?* argues that this entire legend is simply an adaptation of the myth of Tammuz; that Hiram was part of a group of priest-kings and that he was killed by the others, as a voluntary sacrifice, during his consecration of the temple, in order to bring good luck to the building.

Leadbeater also retains from this work of Waed that Hiram Abiff would be identified with Abibaal, father of Hiram, king of Tyre, and even suggests that Hiram was not a personal name at all, but a liter of the kings of Tyre, like Pharaoh was the title of the kings of Egypt.

A rabbinical tradition relates that Solomon ordered the massacre of all those who had helped in the construction of the Temple for fear that they would then build temples to false gods.

Ragon recounts in *Masonic Orthodoxy* the origins of the use of the legend of Hiram in Freemasonry modeled on the

Ancient Mysteries [22]. This text from 1853 is taken up by Papus, in the *Revue l'Initiation* n°1 of 1957 [23]. Here is an excerpt:

"In 1646, a Rosicrucian society, formed according to the ideas of *La* Bacon's *new Atlantis* , assembles in the meeting room of the *free-masons* in London. Elias Ashmole and the other brothers of the Rosicrucians, having recognized that the number of professional workers was surpassed by that of intellectual workers, thought that the time had come to renounce the formulas for receiving these workers, which did not consisted only of a few ceremonies roughly similar to those used among all professional people, which had, until then, served as a shelter for initiates to gain followers . They replaced them, by means of the oral traditions which they used for aspirants to the occult sciences, with a written mode of initiation modeled on the ancient mysteries and those of Egypt and Greece. The first initiatory grade was written approximately as we know it. This first degree having received the approval of the initiates, the rank of companion was drawn up in 1648 and that of master shortly after. But the beheading of Charles I [in] 1649 and the side that Ashmole took in favor of the Stuarts brought major modifications to this third and last rank which had become biblical.

Robert Vallery-Radot, in an article in the journal *Les documents maçonniques* of October 1942, accepts Brother Lantoine's supposition attributing its origin to the Rosicrucians: the legend of Hiram "could be Stuartist masons who invented it, hiding under this symbol their pain and their hope of revenge. Under this myth they would have mourned their sovereign beheaded by Cromwell. They

---

[22]JM Ragon *Masonic Orthodoxy 1853* : <tinyurl.com/histoire-grades>.
[23]Revue L'Initiation, p.3: < tinyurl.com/Initiation-1957-1 >.

would have called themselves sons of the widow, that is to say of Henriette de France, widow of Charles Stuart. The lost word that they would have sought would have been the son of the deceased king .

For Pierre Noël, "the antecedents of hiramic drama must be sought in the *Mystery plays* , these scenes of biblical inspiration played in the Middle Ages first in churches, then on the squares, before being played in different places of the city. They were generally played in cycles. We have kept several which were played in York, Wakefield, Norwich or London. Reserved for the major moments of the liturgical year, these representations were often entrusted to trade bodies, guilds or corporations, which financed them and ensured their production. Hence their name mystery or *mystery* , from Latin *misterium* (meaning occupation) or *ministerium* (occupation or *craft* in English). Their subject was biblical passages such as Creation, the fault of Adam and Eve, the murder of Abel, the construction of Noah's ark, the flood, the visit of the wise men, the massacre of the innocents, the judgment last. That is to say that themes close to the legend of Hiram (death, violence, the temple of Jerusalem, etc.) were present in these medieval dramas, associated directly or indirectly with trades [24].

For the record, in the *Graham manuscript* of 1726, three legends are narrated there , the third concerns Hiram completing the Temple but not dying a violent death. It was only in 1730, against a backdrop of religious opposition, that the Grand Lodge of England, predominantly Anglican, replaced the dead body of Noah with the corpse of a murder, Hiram. Thus, through Anglican ideology, the legend of Hiram obscured the Calvinist interpretation, even

---

[24] Pierre Noël, *Anodine reflections on the rank of Maître* : <tinyurl.com/le-grade-de-maitre>.

going so far as to identify the Calvinists with the assassins of the master builder.

The legend, which will become the founding myth of speculative Freemasonry and the probable origin of the 3rd degree , is only described for the first time in 1730, in *Masonry Dissected* by Prichard, a text interweaving the story of the legend with indications of ritual practices. The importance of Prichard's disclosure is not only in revealing for the first time a three-grade system, culminating with the master's grade, *The Master's Part* , its profound originality was in proposing the first known and coherent version of the legend which, from now on, constitutes the heart of the rank of master.

A hypothesis of the objective of this legend, formulated by Henrik Bogdan in the text *The cabalistic influence on the development of the degree of Master in Freemasonry* : " it seems obvious that, in its original form, it was a myth of initiation, unlike more recent versions in which the legend adopts the function of a moralistic story.
The relationship to the cabalistic tradition manifests itself more visibly when the initiatory aspect of the legend is highlighted. At the heart of Jewish cabalism lies the fundamental goal of individual experience of God or *unio mystica.* It is this fundamental purpose that functionally links the two traditions . Both of these traditions lead to a direct identification with God or an experience of God [25].

The legend of Hiram itself stops here for the blue lodges of the continental rites, but it has extensions in the degree of master among the Anglo-Saxons as well as in certain High Masonic Ranks which relate, in particular, the manner in

---

[25]Henrik Bogdan , The cabalistic influence on the development of the degree of Master in Freemasonry, p.48: <academia.edu/1601260/>.

which the guilty will be punished and the continuation of the construction of the Temple of Solomon.

Agricol Perdiguier, journeyman carpenter, about the Duty practiced by the Children of Solomon wrote in 1839: "An old fable is spread about them where it is a question of Hiram according to some, or of Adoniram according to others ; we see crimes and punishments there, but I leave this fable for what it is worth.

We will consult the texts dealing with the legend of Hiram (in chronological order) on the best documented site [26].

Various hypotheses, circumstances or concepts have been evoked from this legend: the real death of Hiram Abif; the myth of Osiris; an allegory of the setting sun; the expulsion of Adam from paradise; the death of Abel; Noah's entry into the Ark; the annual path of the sun punctuated by the equinoxes and solstices (the three murderers would then be the three months of the year when the sun declines); the death and resurrection of Mithra of the Persians, Bacchus of the Greeks and Atys of the Phrygians, whose passion these people celebrated; the death and resurrection of Christ, the three assassins of Master Hiram being none other than the Jewish high priest Caiaphas, the king of Galilee Herod, and the Roman governor of Judea Pontius Pilate; the persecution of the Templars and the death of Jacques de Molay; the death of Charles I [Stuart] ; an allegory invented by Cromwell against the Stuarts; the murder of Archbishop of Canterbury Thomas Becket; an invention of the Jacobites to help the House of Stuart; a representation of the Golden Age ; the drama of generation-regeneration; the resurrection as a general dogma; the descent of Aeneas into Hades; the revolt of Korè, Dathan and Abiram against Moses; Adoram,

---

[26] The site documented on Hiram: <tinyurl.com/documents-Hiram>.

King Rehoboam's taxman; the legend of Christian Rosenkreutz; shamanic initiation rites (particularly in Siberia and Australia); the WORK of the Black in the alchemical process of preparing the philosopher's stone (according to René Guénon, Hiram is the symbolic transposition of the *Materia Prima* of the alchemists); the equivalence between Hermes (Trismegistus) and Hiram. Hutchinson, the first philosophical writer on Freemasonry in England, supposes that it was intended to embody the idea of the decadence of the Jewish religion and the substitution of Christianity in its place and over its ruins.

Ragon makes Hiram a symbol of the sun stripped of its life-giving rays and fruit-giving power during the three months of winter, and of its restoration to generative warmth by the season of spring [27].

Doctor Pierre-Gérard Vassal's hypothesis would be that it was Solomon himself who recorded the story of the three leaders who were put to death for their conspiracy against his father: David, Absalom, Ahithophel and Adonijah. The analysis he makes of this legend can be found in his *Complete Course of Masonry or General History of Initiation: from its origin to its institution in France* [28].

It is certain that, for all Masons of the past, and even today for the vast majority of Masons in regular Masonry, the myth of Hiram represents, if not the Judeo-Christian idea of the resurrection of the body, of minus the spiritualist doctrine of the survival of the person. In any case, we can understand this legend through two different stories, that of the "martyrdom of a hero" on the one hand, and that of the

---

[27] Albert G. Mackey, *The Symbolism of Freemasonry* , chap. XXVII, *The legend of the third degree* : <tinyurl.com/legende-Hiram>.

[28] Pierre-Gérard Vassal, *Complete Masonry Course…*, from p.213: <tinyurl.com/les-conspirateurs>.

"saint founder" on the other hand with a hagiographic aim [with an edifying intention], as Philippe Langlet says.

Character names

Hiram

The word Hiram, in Hebrew, is made up of three letters: *Heth, Resch, Mem* . He is primarily called Hiram, but in 1 Kings 7:40 he is called ח י ר ו מ (Hirom) and in 2 Chronicles 4 he is known as חורם (Huram). 2 Chronicles 4:16 even speaks of Huram-abi.

The cards of the Tarot which correspond to these letters are: *Heth* La Justice, *Resch* Le Judgment, *Mem* La Mort (the fellow). *HiRaM* can also be read in this language as *HaReM* which designates the hidden thing , the dark place or as *Ir'HaM* meaning "high life" or "elevation after death".

For the Rosicrucians, Hiram is believed to be an abbreviation for " *Homo Jesus Redemptor Animarum* ".

Hiram, a mythical character, embodies for Freemasonry a syncretism of these beings who must die to resurrect, to found a current of Tradition. The character of Hiram can lend itself to symbolic interpretations broad enough for all Freemasons to commune with their predecessors from the most diverse times and cults.
The master Hiram, this sublime worker, gifted with intelligence and rare knowledge, nicknamed Hiram Abif, according to the interpreters, means "sent from God". This man, revered by Hiram, King of Tyre, esteemed, cherished, honored by Solomon was the chief conductor of the construction of the first Temple in Jerusalem, he

coordinated the classes of workers according to Freemasonry.

The tribe of Naphtali from which he comes is that of the blacksmiths (1 Kings ; 7,14) who we know are, of all traditions, those who create the world through their mastery of the bowels of the earth. The man Hiram, son of a widow, is presented as the last blacksmith, hypothetical descendant of Tubalcain who was the first. As such , he would be the last bearer of the secrets of creation, the last of the descendants of Noah's brother. This is why the homonymous King sent him to Solomon in order to build the Temple of the Lord (2 Chronicles ; 2,12) because it is very obvious that the descendants of the creator of the Ark, bearer of the first covenant, did not cannot be strangers to the construction of the stone dwelling which will welcome God.
The story of his death and his assassination by three companions is a fiction favored in this respect by the silence of the Scriptures.

Each circumstance of the disastrous event, which the masons commemorate in their work, makes known the virtues to be practiced. His glorious exit from the tomb, which we trace, makes known the reward. Hiram, going assiduously to the Temple to say his prayers, after the workers had retired, taught the masons that in this capacity they owe even more than the others a pure homage to the Supreme Being. Hiram, murdered by three Companions who want to snatch the Master's Word from him in order to usurp his pay, makes known the danger of violent passions which can lead to the greatest disorders if they are not repressed, the injustice of those who, without taking the trouble of doing the necessary work on themselves, would like to snatch their discoveries from others and appropriate the fruits of them. Hiram is the symbol of the man of great valor who, despite temptations and persecutions, achieves victory over his weaknesses and passions, approaching human perfection. He is also the symbol of the man faithful to duty, even if duty is inflexible like fate, demanding like necessity and imperative like destiny. It is, above all, a symbol of the Freemason who prefers to die rather than fail in the task for which he is sworn.

"If the story relates good deeds about good people, the moved listener is encouraged to imitate the good ; and if it evokes bad actions about bad men , nevertheless, the pious and God-fearing listener or reader , avoiding what is criminal and vicious , burns to seek for his part even more skillfully what ' he learned to be good and worthy of God' [29].

Hiram, released from his funerary shroud and emerging gloriously from his tomb, is called to a new life, surrounded by the virtues that he has constantly practiced and which assure him of the immortality to which all those of his avatars who know how to do so must also aspire. 'imitate.
"Hiram is , from an astronomical point of view, the emblem of the sun, the symbol of its apparent progress. Under this allegorical legend lies the expression of the great and profound law of palingenesis which requires the violent death of the initiator as a complement to initiation.
Hiram, the same as Osiris, as Mithra, as Bacchus, as Balder, as all the gods celebrated in the ancient mysteries, is one of the thousand personifications of the sun. Hiram means in Hebrew: high life; which clearly designates the position of the sun in relation to the earth. According to the historian Josephus, Hiram was the son of a Tyrian named Ur, meaning fire.

---

[29] Saint Bede , *The Venerable* **p** . 159 : <tinyurl.com/objectif-moral>

He is also called Hiram-Abi, Hiram father, as the Latins said: *Jovis pater* , Jupin father; *liber pater* , Bacchus father. But then there exists, between Hiram and Hiram-Abi, the same difference as among the Egyptians, for example, between Horus and Osiris. This is the sun which goes out at the winter solstice; this one, the sun which is reborn at the same time [30].

By another Christic interpretation, that of Edouard de Ribaucourt, Hiram would be the anagram of " *Homo Iesus Rex Altissimus Mundi* ".

Hiram, living, respected, cherished and directing the great construction through his talents and knowledge, represents the Order in its primitive state, when it was still known only by its benefits and by the just admiration it inspired. His tragic death indicates the state of the Order, succumbing to the misbehavior of its members designated by three companions under the guise of envy, greed and slander.

We cannot reject the hypothesis that Hiram evokes Sir Christopher Wren, the architect, the *Master of Work,* who rebuilt Saint Paul's (also called The Temple) after the fire of London and where he is buried [31].

The most curious supposition about Hiram's identity was made by the misandre Céline Renooz in her 1925 book [32]*The Era of Truth* , claiming that in fact a woman, the

---

[30]FT Bègue-Clavel, *Picturesque History of Freemasonry* , p.83: <tinyurl.com/Hiram-soleil>.
[31]Marc Labouret, *Christopher Wren, Hiram's model?* : <tinyurl.com/histoire-Wren>
[32]Céline Renooz, *History of human thought, moral evolution of humanity through the ages and among all peoples* : < tinyurl.com/Hiram-femme >.

daughter of the King of Tyre, was hidden beneath the name of Hiram. Based on the Hebrew text of the Bible marked by the feminization of the adjectives which qualify King David, Renooz considers just as curiously that in truth this king was a queen, named Daud, who created the city of Jerusalem and undertook to build the Temple there. "Queen Daud was not alone in founding the secret Institution which was to spread through Freemasonry . She had two collaborators, two Magi Queens (or Magicians), with whom the sacred triptych was formed that the three points of the Order have since represented. One is Balkis, queen of Ethiopia (called the queen of Sheba), the other is a queen of Tyre, who was hidden behind the name Hiram. This queen of Tire being Elissar or Dido ." For Renooz, the legend of Hiram and the ancient traditions provide a glimpse of what Solomon's role was: it was he who attacked and overthrew female power and established male royalty on the ruins of gynecocracy.

From an alchemical point of view Hiram is the one who reads the divine Plans and puts them into action, he is the one who holds from Solomon the organizing Word of the construction site and gives the salt which allows the suffering of the companions to associate with the mercury of the Masters. He is the alchemist behind the construction of the Athanor Temple, the purpose of which intersects with the Philosopher's Stone [33].

The Bible mentions two Adoniram וַאֲדֹנִירָם. One who also participated in the work of the Temple as overseer of the woodcutters of Lebanon (I Kings 5, 28) and another Adoniram וַאֲדֹנִירָם in I Kings, 4 , 6 (which we find in II

---

[33] Scotsman of Saint John, *Legend of Hiram - Anamorphosis of the Master* :
< tinyurl.com/Hiram-alchemical >.

Chronicles 10, 18 under the name of Adhoram הֲדֹרָם), son of Abda, who was murdered during the reign of Rehoboam, son of Solomon, while he was collecting taxes. His name is also written Adoram, Hadoram.

a body of prodigious size was discovered at Sagunto . There was on the stone which covered it, the following inscription, the translation of which is given to us by Billerus Villalpondus who regards it as authentic: HIC EST TUMULUS ADONIRAM SERVI REGIS SALOMONIS QUI VENIT DEMANDET TRIBUTUM MORTUUS EST DIE [34].

We find in the Bible another Hiram (עִירָם), one of the leaders of Edom (Gen, 36:43). Also, two Yhoram often mentioned in the Bible: (Joram, יְהוֹרָם), in particular, one son of Jehoshaphat, king of Judah in 2 Chr, 21; the other son of Ahab, king of Israel in 2Kings, 3.

Hiram Abif

In the Old Charges of English Operative Masonry, the Hiram Abif of Masonic legend is cited several times as being the son of King Hiram of Tyre, under various names: Adoniram, Haram, Aynone, Aman, Aymon, Hymon, Anon or even Adon. Researchers have tried to solve the enigma of the personality and work of the architect of the Temple nicknamed Hiram Abif.

Historian Roger Dachez brings the fruit of his methodical research to discuss the controversial origins of the name given to the great master builder of the Temple. The choice

---

[34] *Masonic Manual or Tuileur of all Masonic rites practiced in France* ,..., 1830, by a veteran of Masonry, supposed to be Claude-André Vuillaume, note 3, p. 60:
< tinyurl.com/inscription-Adoniram >.

of the term Hiram Abif to designate, in Masonic texts, the architect of the Temple of Solomon, opens up a questioning. The expression Hiram Abi or Abiv is in fact found in only two places in the Bible: firstly in 2Chronicles 2,12 where we can read Huram Abi (אֲבִי חוּרָם); "So I am sending you a skillful man, full of knowledge, Houram Abi." Secondly in 2Chr ;4,16, where we have Huram Abiv (אָבִיו חוּרָם) "All these utensils that King Solomon made at Huram Abiv for the house of the Lord were of polished brass".

From these simple data, questions arise: The root ab means father, abi has a determinative which means my father; as for abiv, it means his father. Consequently, from a purely philological point of view, these terms mean: Houram my father (Houram abi), Houram his father (Houram abiv), two rather enigmatic expressions. However, we must remember that a broader meaning of father, in Hebrew, can indicate the notion of master, instructor, leader or advisor, and translated as such in the Hebrew/French Bible of Mechon.

We find in the Bible another Huram (חוּרָם) descended from Benjamin through his daughter Bella, I Chr. .8.5) .

In I Kings 7.13 which is the third biblical place where we speak of our Hiram, the craftsman, not the King, it should be noted that it is indeed Hiram, and not Huram, that it is absolutely not Hiram-Abi or Hiram Abif, but simply Hiram (חִירָם), who comes from Tyre, the text specifying that he is the son of a Tyrian and a widow from the tribe of Naphtali (This writing, which can be translated by Hiram, is reserved, in all the other verses of the Bible, where it appears, to Hiram king of Tyre). Moreover, in this book, it is exclusively a bronze worker, who will cast the columns, the bronze sea of the Temple, but in no way an architect nor a stonemason.

The two preceding remarks suggest that we are apparently describing two significantly different characters, especially since the skills of Houram abi, in 2Chronicles ;2,13 , are much more extensive. He was a man gifted for all kinds of work, knowing how to work with "gold, silver, bronze, iron, stone, wood, scarlet, purple, engrave anything and everything. invent everything. This Huram is a character very similar to that of Bezaléel. The biblical text brings the art of Huram closer to that of Bezaléel (whose legend is mentioned in the *Graham Manuscript*): It is thanks to 3 virtues that the first temple was built by Bezaléel as it is written in Exodus 31.3 : "I [god] have filled him with the spirit of Elohim in wisdom, in understanding and in knowledge", וּבְדַעַת וּבִתְבוּנָה בְּחָכְמָה, virtues that we find in Hiram in I King 7, 14 "filled with wisdom, of intelligence and knowledge" הַדַּעַת-וְאֶת הַתְּבוּנָה-וְאֶת הַחָכְמָה -אֶת וַיִּמָּלֵא. Note, also, that they were both of the tribe of Dan. The three virtues, concepts, divine attributes, types of forces, levels of consciousness, processes at work in living structures, the 3 sephiroth retained are: Hokhmah, wisdom, (heith, kaph, mem, heh, i.e. 8 +20+40+5=67); Tébouna, alias Binah, intelligence (tav, beith, vav, noun, hey, i.e. 400+2+6+50+5=463); Daath, knowledge, knowledge (daleth, eïn, tav, i.e. 4+70+400=474). By adding these virtues we obtain 67+463+474=1004, or in reduced value 5, the same as that of the addition of the divine presence (shekhina, שכינה,300+20+10+50+5 =385) and of the sacred Temple, the mishkan, (משכן) 40+300+20+700 = 1060) which equals 385+1060=1445, in reduced value 5.

If Hiram, in the Books of Kings, was only a bronze worker, Houram Abi from the Book of Chronicles is much more eclectic and possibly knows how to work stone. However, he remains a craftsman, and not the Master Mason of the Temple, as indicated, and only by them, in the Ancient

Duties. (Hiram would not designate a particular personê but a function, that of the foremen descendants of Tubal-Caïn and dispensers of a secret Cainite tradition transmitted from generation to generation since it was founded, on the land of Nod where the children of Cain, the very first city that the Bible called Henokia .''

We can thus think that the Hiram Abif of the Masonic tradition, who only appears in the texts in 1723, is a composite character, borrowing from two quite different portraits, and who is not found, as such, in no biblical text. It only became in 1730, with Anglican Freemasonry as it appears in Prichard's *Masonry Dissected* , the only mythical referent of the rank of master, supplanting Noah and Bezaléel.
We find neither in Kings, nor in Chronicles, Ezekiel, Jeremiah, nor in the writings of Flavius Josephus nor in the rabbinical commentaries any report on the death of Hiram (Abif).

The book The Key of Hiram relates: King Sekenenre was fighting a great mental battle with Apophis, the Hyksos king, so he needed the full power of the sun god Amun-Re to give him the strength to be victorious. Sitting in Thebes, he left the royal palace of Malkata every day to go to the temple of Amun-Re at high noon, when the sun was at its zenith and a man cast practically no shadow or shadow. area of darkness on the ground. When the sun was at its zenith, the power of Ra reached its apex and that of the god Apophis, its lowest point. The secrets of the Egyptian royal coronation disappeared with Sekenenrê, the man whom authors Chistopher Knight and Robert Lomas call Hiram Abif (the lost king). When the mummy of Sekenenrê Taâ was discovered in 1881, it was obvious that he had met a violent end. The middle of his forehead had been crushed, another blow had fractured his right eye socket, his right cheekbone and his nose. A third blow was struck behind his left ear ' shattering his mastoid and ending in the first vertebra of his neck. Sekenenrê was killed because he did not want to reveal the secrets of the royal coronation to the Hyksos.

6 THE ASSUMPTION OF THE MASTER

It is in the silence and in the chthonic darkness, under the shroud, that the elevation of the companion to the rank of Master germinates. This ceremony centers on the assassination of a mythical character, Hiram, and his recovery [35].

The first problem is that of the choice of the character Hiram as designating the architect whose drama is revealed to us, in Freemasonry, in the famous disclosure of Samuel Prichard, *La Maçonnerie Dissquée* , published in London in 1730 [36].

Then comes the problem of the connection of this drama of the Master Masons with the Great and Small Mysteries [37]. We can naturally assign various mythological sources to this legend and find, by searching a little in the history of ancient peoples and ancient religions, Egyptian, Greco-Roman, even Celtic, a number of sacred stories and myths which can constitute as many models.

The rituals corresponding to this Death-Resurrection were called, in ancient Egypt, "The Door of Death". In modern

---

[35] Do not hesitate to read Papus' article, *The Legend of Hiram* , in issue 1 of 1957 of the *Revue L'initiation* : <tinyurl.com/L-Initiation-1957-1>.

[36] < tinyurl.com/maonnerie-dissequee >.

[37] < tinyurl.com/mysteries-grands-et-petits >.

Masonic rituals, Osiris is replaced by Hiram who nevertheless remains very bearer of the same solar meanings...

Inventor or expert in the arts, blacksmith, builder, archetype of the Creative Man and whose very name means "high", "greatness". Killing Hiram and making him reborn means that the Sun loses its strength in Winter to return to Spring... The cycle of births can then resume... One word replaces another, one breath replaces another... and the "sacrifice" is consummated... HRM is the archetype of all the saviors of humanity, likewise, it is also that of human continuity and its creative spirit. Like Odin, he is the God crucified on the World Tree or asleep at the heart of its roots.

We also wondered about what would have happened if the legend had not ended, as Prichard relates it in *Dissected Masonry* , with a lost word, a substituted word and an architect tragically disappeared. Indeed, we can easily see the flaw in this diagram: we will have to find the lost word and replace the architect. Here is enough to write five or six other legends and as many new grades. If masonry immediately launched itself, and for several decades, into a prodigious and sometimes crazy enterprise creating grades in search of the lost Word, is it not simply because the authors of the founding legend constructed it as an open and unfinished story?

He who is at the bottom of the valley has a representation of it. When he climbs the mountainside, the view becomes very different. Each time he makes a station at a higher height, his panorama changes. Likewise , we can understand that from a higher perspective, the world of yesterday's objects enters a radically new perspective. The silence which surrounds the tomb of the Master, beyond Death, offers the renewal of language, the sharing of new terms, another form of breaking the silence.

" *If I felt the same today as yesterday, I would lose the will to live* " as Rabbi Nachman of Bratslav said .

The recovery, the assumption , is the work of the respectable Master of the lodge assisted by the two supervisors.

After being literally knocked out by the fatal blow of the third companion's mallet, buried under the mound, then found, the master is raised to life, exalted. So can we talk about assumption ?

Assumption comes from " *ad+sumere* ", to take with oneself, to add someone, something. We find this etymology in assume. In logic, it is the act of adding a hypothesis to reasoning. In theology: It is the elevation-resurrection of Mary helped by her son. Resurrecting Christ alone makes the Ascension, but Mary, with help, does the Assumption.

Etymology would allow us **to do this based on the word SUM and its different meanings** :
~   Sleep comes, like its cousin sleep, from the god Somnus , the Roman equivalent of the Greek Hypnos 38, twin brother of Thanatos, the god of death.
~   The sum, derived from summus , the highest point, designates the result of an addition, and is similar to summit, summit, pinnacle.

---

[38]Homer's Iliad (translation by Leconte de Lisle) song 14:
<tinyurl.com/Homere-chant14 >.

~　　the sum, coming from sagma , the load, the pack, designates, under the expression beast of burden, the animal which carries the burdens.

~　　The verb to knock out is similar to sleep-to-sleep. To knock someone out is to put them to sleep. Except that the word initially had the meaning of moral dejection, and only later took on the meaning of killing, then that of suddenly putting one to sleep. Some believe it actually comes from sagma , the beast of burden. To knock down would then be to be overwhelmed under a burden. The word would have derived meaning by etymological contagion with sleep-sleep.

The idea of sleep has been found since the first centuries of the church, both among the Latins and the Greeks in the expression **dormitio** to mean death, and even... the feast of the Assumption of the Virgin.

Synthesizing these etymologies , the recovery of the master, at the same time stunned, asleep, carried to the summit, resurrected and welcomed by the respectable Master assisted by the two supervisors, cannot be akin to an assumption? And in this case, in this psychopomp mission, as in the images of the dormition of the saints, our first three officers became angels (smiles!) .

" On this Assumption Day, the heavens received the blessed Virgin with joy. The Angels rejoice, the Archangels jubilant, the Thrones come alive, the Dominions celebrate it in canticles, the Principalities unite their voices, the Powers accompany with their musical instruments, the Cherubim and the Seraphim intone hymns . Like the celestial entities, do not acclamations exalt joy at the advent?

And the master is reborn more radiant than ever.

Yes, I know where I come from! Unsatisfied, like the flame, I burn [I am burning] to consume myself. What I hold becomes light, coal what I leave: For I am certainly flame! [39]
It is not in the mysticism of religions, which only has a theological scope, that I seek the meaning of this sentence, but rather in the mysticism of initiations which essentially has a metaphysical scope.

From the ancient Egyptians to us, **man has always believed to conceal in the highest and most luminous part of himself, a principle different from the body, which controls him and survives him** . Divine fire, according to the Stoics; bit of divinity among Christians. Always the same intuition of a superior, and specifically human, essence, considered immortal by way of hope, as with Socrates, or certainty as with Jesus. Everything suggests that the Masonic representation of death ends in something other than nothingness, leading us into a dualistic spiritualist fiction of mind/body. If the master is reborn, there is therefore a continuation of death, a gradual progression which seems to prepare for the material death of the mason for a rebirth in spirit in a fight against morphological disorganization.

From another angle, by convergence, **emerging from alchemical putrefaction** , Hiram comes back to life more radiant than he was before, as the sentence suggests. Philosophers call *bodies* what they also call *metals* . More radiant than ever, the White Work has been created. The smelting of metals is considered death. For alchemy, treating the *materia prima* in a crucible (crux) is called "crucifying" it. The sulfur extracted represents virtue, that is to say the core or spirit of metal.

---

[39] Frédéric Nietzsche , *Le Gai Savoir, Ecce homo* , par. 62: <tinyurl.com/Le-Gai-Savoir>.

The glorious body is the body of immortality. From Christianity (glorious body) to Taoism (rainbow body), this " *new birth* " is the normal goal of any authentic spiritual path. In the Rite of Egyptian High Masonry, the white alb (or the white habit) is the image of this glorious body.

In the Judeo-Christian tradition, the idea of the glorious body is based on interpretations of an Old Testament verse which says: "Yahweh God made for the man and his wife coats of skin and clothed them with them" (Genesis 3, 21). Very early on, some exegetes thought that the tunic referred to in this verse is made of their own skin which covers the beings of light that they were before. For this, they relied on the fact that in Hebrew the words skin, âur (ע ו ר) light , aur (אור) are similar. Note that in Hebrew , the word â our, to wake up, is written with the same letters as that of the skin (ע ו ר). The skin apron would then represent the "skin clothes" with which man has put on in passing from the spiritual to the biological. In Kabbalah, in the world of Atzilouth, the world of emanation, the soul is enveloped in light (אור, Aur, Kabbalistic term for divine emanation and influence. Due to its properties, it is the favorite Kabbalistic metaphor of the Divine influence; by the Sephirotic principle of the densification of light, this envelope becomes in the world of Assiah, the lower world of action, the skin (עור, â ur). This passage allows to interpret the skin tunics with which Adam and Eve are dressed in Genesis ; a theory taken up by Martin ès de Pasqually in his Treatise *on* Reintegration .

Psychodrama dissociates our being into two parts: that of shadow and matter, impure and corrupt like metals which will be buried in a pit or a mausoleum; that of the spirit which will fly away from all contingency to join this founding center like a phoenix. The use of ornithological symbols has been known to us since the apprentice grade with the Rooster, symbol of awakening linked to the App, then the hawk, symbol of the quest for the peaks, but still terribly material which is , him, linked to the Comp agnon, and finally the Phoenix who achieved Unity.

The phoenix , this mythical bird with scarlet plumage, of incomparable beauty, which, after having lived several centuries (400 or 500 years), immolated itself on a pyre and was reborn, like a sun, from its ashes. Its origin comes from the sacred Egyptian bird Benou (it was the historian Herodotus who introduced it into Western mythology), a gray heron who was the first being to land on the original hill resulting from the silt. He embodied the god of the sun in Heliopolis, his worshipers said that he only appeared every 500 years. It is also reported that the phoenix fed exclusively on dew and that he brought fragrant herbs from distant regions to place them on the altar of Heliopolis, with the aim of igniting them to reduce himself to ashes. . He was reborn 3 days later. Its connection with the regeneration of life comes from its association with the daily cycle of the sun and the annual cycle of the Nile floods. For the Greeks, Benu became the Phoenix (*phoinix*) whose name perhaps comes from the Egyptian verb *wbn* which means "to shine", "sparkle" and "to be born" concerning the Sun.

In Jewish legends it is called **Milcham** . The explanation for his immortality comes from Eve who, after tasting the fruit of the forbidden tree, also succeeds in tempting the animals and making them taste the fruit too. Only the bird Milcham did not give in to temptation, for this the angel of death obedient to God offered him the reward of never making him know the experience of death. Since then, every thousand years, the bird burns; All that remains is an egg which turns into a chick and the bird continues to live.

This bird is not the only one not to know death; it was taught: the thirteen who never tasted death are: Milc ḥ am the bird and his generation : Enoch son of Jared, Serah daughter of Yashar, Bithiah the daughter of Pharaoh , Javetz, Hiram king of Tyre, Elijah, the servant of the king of Ethiopia , the Messiah, and the generation of Yonadav son of Rekhev, the grandson of R. Yehudah the Prince, R. Yehoshua b . Levi, and Eliezer, Abraham's servant.

The phoenix is the culmination of the Work, symbol of the secret fire, which "creates" in the philosopher's stone, giving it its red color. Assimilated by alchemists to philosophical sulfur and the number four (the four elements of the physical stone and the four stages of transmutation), the Phoenix represents the fixity of the living being in its continual death, source of spontaneous rebirth. In alchemy, the egg represents chaos as the adept understands it, the prima materia in which the soul of the world is captive. From the egg – symbolized by the round cooking vessel – flies the eagle or the phoenix, the liberated soul.

The first Christians, for their part, made it one of the symbols of the resurrection. The Easter sublimation of the egg (passage, resurrection, immortality) is now identified with the symbolism of the bird which is reborn from its ashes. The Easter egg symbolizes this principle of renewal.

The phoenix is one of the major symbols of the entire Rectified Scottish Rite, accompanied by the motto *Perit Ut Vivat* , "he dies that he may live." The Phoenix is the emblem of the Novice Squires of the Rectified Scottish Regime, it is also the oldest symbol of masonry because it is the image of honor which perishes only to revive and of the

Order which has perished in the flames only to be reborn immediately from his ashes.

The Stoics made the phoenix the symbol of the periodic conflagration of the universe, followed by regeneration.

The image of this legendary animal encourages us to burn our inadequacies and be reborn from the ashes of the old man.

Extend the approach to this mythical animal with the text on this subject by Prof. Christian Ghasarian, *The Rebirth of the Phoenix, Myth(s) and symbol(s)* [40].

We find this ontological meaning in the Hebrews' exodus from Egypt. The Pharaoh archetype represents absolute selfishness in the Torah. In Pharaoh there is nothing spiritual, the higher soul does not accompany him; it does not illuminate. Pharaoh is considered in Kabbalah as a vegetative (or animal) soul which does not shine; it represents at the individual level the evil inclination; the *Yetzer HaRa'* . Indeed, when the creature repairs its Paro level; he leaves Metzarim, from its limits (another reading of Mizraim, Egypt). The light of interiority is represented by Moses in the biblical story; he is the force of altruistic desire. It is the higher level of the soul that illuminates. It begins above the *Nefesh* (the vegetative soul); starting from the *Rua'h* , the breath or the spirit, then, it is the *Neshamah* , the soul itself. The initials of *Neshamah* and *Roua'h* (the 2nd and 3rd levels of the soul) teach us; they reveal the word *Nér* (Noun-Reich), light, opposed to the opacity of Pharaoh.

The serpent is also a symbol of the light of all rebirth . Indeed, just like the snake that sheds its old skin to take on a new skin, the "divine and immortal" consciousness in

---

[40] Christian Ghasarian, *The Rebirth of the Phoenix* :
<academia.edu/3520654>.

each of us rejects a personality at each death to take another rebirth. It is the luminous symbol that represents the cycle of many lives of a human being and **their progression in the mutation of their consciousness.**

How to interpret this light of the new master?

After knowing the world in its differences, its manifestations, its colors, with a knowledge of shadow, the master knows it in its unity with a knowledge of light. When Hiram returns to the world, the curtains of the gloomy room open and let in the light, that of life, the original light freed from the dross accumulated during previous wanderings. The lodge is reformed in the Middle Chamber of the master masons, a very illuminated place as it is said in the Ritual: "The lodge finds the Glorious Body, become Body of Light containing space / time / universe / body of light / body of life." Implicitly, it is the stopping of the chain of lives and deaths, of karma, it is liberation.

Light, enlightenment, for Emmanuel Kant, is man's exit from the state of tutelage for which he himself is responsible (the state of tutelage is the inability to use his understanding without the conduct of another). The master is a responsible being, removed from this state of supervision.

Hiram's death is necessary for him to permeate us. The master is then like a bird that Nerval calls the elusive living flame. Light cannot rot, it is not of the order of the visible but, like the mind, it can show order ab chaos. When a red giant star dies, it destroys its entire solar system with all the planets it contained. But this destructive act releases the dust of life into space. These chemical particles released in vast quantities will spread life elsewhere. So, let's not forget that we are made up of protons which rotate at the speed of light, and like a giant star the master knows the junction, the contact between body and light.

According to Christian theology: "It is God the Son Himself, the Word of God, who resurrects Himself from his dead body. His soul therefore resurfaces and the glorious form of this body victoriously reanimates His corpse. He is the Mediator in His body of His resurrection." For alchemy, treating the *materia prima* in a crucible (crux) is called "crucifying" it.

The halo is in some way a prefiguration of the resurrection, particularly of the saints [41], in a glorious body; according to Origen, this resurrection body would have the shape of a sphere.

For Paracelsus, man is understood according to his three bodies, *but also according to three spirits which are three lights* . The first of these spirits is the one who animates our visible body of flesh and blood. It is thanks to it that natural functions are accomplished : nutrition, procreation. The second of the three spirits is the one who reigns in our invisible sidereal body and who is one with it. It is located at the level of our thinking, our active imagination. It is the sidereal spirit. Finally, the third spirit identifies with the glorious body, also invisible, generated by the Holy Spirit.

The Sun is the prototype of the dead who is reborn every morning .

The new master is imperishable because he is identified with the luminous totality, "He is more radiant than ever". This expression also expresses the solar aspect of the Rite. Hiram is of the solar type: his rite takes place from sunset to dawn,

---

[41] Dominique Clairambault, *Spiritual flesh and glorious body in Martinism* : <tinyurl.com/corps-glorieux>.

from the death of the sun to its awakening. Cosmic symbol, through assimilation to solar light.

In the Masonic ritual, Hiram represents the Sun, more ideally the Light, that spoken of at the beginning of Genesis and that of the Gospel of Saint John: light of the spirit, supreme intelligence, knowledge of the thing in itself . By substituting the recipient for the slain hero, Hiram reissues the myth of reintegration, that is to say the return to unity which allows what is scattered to be brought together.

When Hiram returns to the world, the curtains of the gloomy room open and let in the light, that of life, the original light freed from the dross accumulated during previous wanderings. The lodge is reformed in the Middle Chamber of the master masons, a very illuminated place as it is said in the Ritual: "The lodge finds the Glorious Body, become Body of Light containing space / time / universe / body of light / body of life." Implicitly, it is the stopping of the chain of lives and deaths, of karma, it is liberation.

It is a liberation identical to that of all bardic, Egyptian, Tibetan funeral rites, etc. The new master is the living liberated, he has known both sides of the same coin : that of life, that of death [42].

A certain number of themes remain to be studied further, of which here are some subjects:
· The relationship between the upper triad and the quaternary base which makes it possible to establish the archetypal Man on the basis of the septenary...
· Incarnation through sacrifice. · The master's lodge board.
· The ontological symbolism of the Temple of Solomon. · The acacia. · The tools used to kill HiRaM. · The spiritual significance of the Master's word which was revealed to you

---

[42] Complete with the text *Hiram's Double Body* by Jean-Bernard Lévy: <academia.edu/11788186>.

with your elevation and its origin through the ancient texts of Freemasonry. · Resurrection, reincarnation, symbolic death. · The enigma of Hiram and his murder, the mystery of his name and the reasons for this choice. · And other themes of study towards which each person's spirituality will lead…

7 MASONIC INVESTIGATION INTO HIRAM'S ASSASSINS

**Hiram's story begins
truly by his assassination.**

"The Masonic journey takes you from the test of the mirror to that of Hiram's death, from individual awareness of your mistakes, faults, and intimate crimes, to collective awareness of the inevitability of the bad companion in everyone."[43]

Humanity did not yet know how to speak, it had already learned to kill. All civilizations, in their founding myths, as in their symbolic legends, were built on transcendent, because demiurgic, murders.

But here it is: the "savagery" of the prehistoric people would only be a myth forged during the second half of the 19th century to reinforce the concept of "civilization" and the discourse on the progress accomplished since the origins. The miserabilist vision of "cruel dawns" is being replaced today — particularly with the development of cultural relativism — by the equally mythical vision of a "golden age". The reality of our ancestors' lives probably fell somewhere in between. As archaeological data shows, compassion and mutual aid, as well as cooperation and solidarity, more than competition and aggression, were

---

[43] Annick Drogou, Jean-Marc Pétillot, *Dictionary of Freemasonry,* 2019, with the word **Guilty** , ..., Numérilivre Eds.

probably key factors in the evolutionary success of our species [44].

In the Freudian vision, becoming an adult is a long apprenticeship. "You must, in stages: kill your gods, kill your masters, kill your parents, kill your brothers, finally kill your peers. This is becoming a man, my son." In *Totem and Taboo* , Sigmund Freud theorizes about ancient times in which a savage horde was led by a tyrannical patriarch, who owned all the women. His brothers rebelled and killed him. But, overcome with guilt, they then worshiped him and founded religion, even culture, on remorse for this murder. Freud elaborates this myth in order to found a phylogenesis (relationship) of the Oedipus complex.

Following in the footsteps of René Girard, the Passion of the Christ, revealing the victim for what he is, a persecuted, an innocent, begins a truly human story, that is to say devoid of this compulsion to violence and to the repression induced by the impossibility of a solution. It is more than a "deconstruction" as Girard likes to say, it is a real ravage of conceptual destruction. Through Christ, non-violence has become possible and, for our civilization, magical, mythical, unconscious behavior can be overcome by the mechanism of persecution brought to light thanks to the analysis of the mimetic principle. There is no need to resort to Freudian concepts which can be avoided.
Yet this message of love has been betrayed by 2000 years of crimes, terror, repression on the black page of Christianity [45].

---

[44] Le Monde Diplomatique, Marylène Patou Mathis, *No , men have not always waged war* : <tinyurl.com/Hommes-et-violences>.

[45] Enrico Riboni, *The black page of Christianity 2000 years of crimes, terror, repression* : <tinyurl.com/Page-noire-christianisme>.

The origin of the word assassin is disputed. The term assassin comes from the Persian name *Hašišyun* which designated the members of a militant Muslim sect, also called Nizârites, particularly active in the 11th [century] in Persia, who publicly assassinated their opponents; these men were called *Fédavi* , that is to say those who sacrifice themselves. They were dressed in white like the followers of Mocanaa in Transoxane three centuries before, and the Christian neophites before them.

Their charismatic leader was Hassan ibn al-Sabbah, the Elder of the Mountain; its government was neither nor should be that of a kingdom or principality; it was a brotherhood, an order. The articles of faith and the duties of an Assassin (collected in a catechism entitled *Askhinaï-risk, Knowledge of his Vocation*) had no basis other than simple allegories; they taught him to consider only the practice of interior worship as essential, and to view with indifference the observation or violation of the laws of religion and morality; he must therefore doubt everything, and have as a principle that nothing was forbidden.

Frequently mentioned, assassin comes from the Arabic *haschashin* , those who smoke hashish or cannabis. Hashish is a drug, Hassan ibn al-Sabbah would have used it to condition his disciples. He intoxicated some of his associates with this plant, promising them that, if they died in his service, they would obtain the felicities of which they had just had a foretaste. However, it is not certain that this practice existed.

According to others, the term derives from the Arabic *assassiyoune* which means "one who monitors", those who are faithful to the Asās, the foundation of faith. This would be the name that Hassan ibn al-Sabbah used to designate his disciples.

In the 13th century, the word passed into Italian under the form *assassino* to designate a Muslim leader fighting Christians, then a hitman. In the 16th century, the word passed into French with this meaning to designate any person paid to commit murder.

For the troubadours this word described blind loving fidelity .

Although human beings do not have, unlike animals, natural brakes on inter-species aggression, they necessarily have the intuition that crime is not a noble act, because in ultimately, as Seneca said, man is a sacred thing for man. Furthermore, at the level of this perception, the human being is aware of the fact that benevolence and respect for others are the conditions of social coexistence; there cannot be existence without coexistence. Aristotle also recalls that man is an animal which is not intended to live in solitude, which refers to the existence of a social order reproducing itself according to the logic of the conventional and not through a system of beliefs. . This is what is called the ethical In-Itself of the world, or the ethical substance of the human. The legal community is the very condition for its accomplishment. "The State of justice cannot create the conditions for the reign of Good at the universal level, without the emergence of axiological consciousness in its fullness, capable of carrying out its work of truth and justice ." Consequently, it is a question not only of recognizing what is, but also of condemning all systems of values and actions which have denied the universality of otherness and produced the universality of crime.

And in this case we should expect that Hiram's killers will be tried and convicted.

At the York Rite, the execution of the 3 evil companions, Hiram's assassins, is part of the 3rd degree ceremony. This theme is only developed in the 9th, 10th and 11th degrees of the REAA.

But who are or what are these bad companions?

We find, in a roughly analogous way throughout all the Hiramian Masonic rites, the story of bad companions which can be narrated in this way.

The bad companions who were accustomed to slipping among the masters to receive the salary, seeing themselves frustrated by Hiram's organization for the pay, resolved to obtain it at whatever cost. And seeing clearly that they could only have it by having the word, the pass and the touch of the master, they held council together on the way they would go about capturing it. They found no other way than to have it given to them willingly or by force and decided to extract the password from Hiram or to assassinate him. They wait for him at the exit of the temple and as Hiram presents himself at the West Gate, the mason tries to force him to reveal the secret. Hiram refuses, he is hit on the shoulder with a ruler. Hiram flees towards the Porte du Midi where the carpenter, after the same scenario, gives him a blow with a lever or a square. Hiram flees once again towards the Orient Gate where the miner finishes him off with a blow from a mallet. The three accomplices took the body to a secluded place where they buried it, then they dug two other graves, one for his clothes, the other for his cane. The objects used to strike the Master were not metal weapons (they were prohibited within the Temple), but tools made of wood or cardboard.

Does this epopty only evoke an imperious desire to monopolize what the companions ignore or only consider

from the strictly material angle "a salary", thus demonstrating their lack of perseverance, patience as much as discernment and real abilities?
There are three typical rebels: the rebel against nature, the rebel against science, the rebel against truth. They were represented in the hell of the Ancients by the three heads of Cerberus. They are figured in the Bible by Korah, Dathan and Abiron. The Templars call them Squin de Florian, Noffo Dei and the unknown who betrayed them.

According to the doctrine of the masters, the bad companions are also ambition, lies and ignorance, or else error, fanaticism and pride. They are also envy, avarice and pride: envy, which poisons all enjoyment and seeks to destroy that of our neighbor; avarice, which often makes us unjust and almost always insensitive to the misfortunes of others; pride, which gets irritated by everything and never forgives (in Antiquity this had a name: hubris , ὕβρις , it was the greatest crime punished by the punishment of Nemesis, divine and irrevocable since it results in the pure and simple annihilation of the individual) . Fateful passions by which man is often blinded.

In the legend of Masonic Hiram, the scoundrels are designated by names which vary according to the rites; we find Jubelas, Jubelos, Jubelum (*Guide of Scottish Masons* 1810: "Jubelas, at the south gate. Jubelos, at the west gate. Jubelum, at the east gate" "(not to be confused with Jubel and Jubal, the sons of Lamech).

Sekenenrê, refusing to reveal the secret allowing him to be resurrected to divine life who would then have the human role of pharaoh, that is to say, representative of God to serve as a link between the Creator and humanity, was murdered.A young priest named Jubelo allegedly allowed the assassins to enter the temple where Pharaoh was. Inspired by this story, Chistopher Knight and Robert Lomas, in their book *The Key of Hiram,* equate Sekenenrê Taâ to Hiram Abif.

We also find for the assassins the names of Holem, Sterkin and Hoterfut, or Abiram, Miphiboseth from the name of a ridiculous and crippled pretender to the kingship of David (*History of magic* , Eliphas Levi, 1860), Phanor, Amrou and Habirama (which means the one who overthrows the father) the miner, also called Méthoushaël , by his other name Hoben, apprentices or journeymen, from different trades, furious at having been refused mastery. The ritual of the 10th ^{degree} of the REAA names them in the presence of their corpses: in the East a skeleton representing Abiram Akyrop (sometimes called Jubulum Akyrop or Hoben); to the West a skeleton representing Sterkin (sometimes called Jubella Guibs); to the South a skeleton representing Oterfut (sometimes called Jubello Gravelot).

Mackey, in his *Encyclopedia* writes at the word *Assassins of the Third Degree* [46]: we have the three "JJJ" in the York and the American rites. In the Adonhiramite system we have Romvel, Plover, and Abiram. In the Scottish Rite we find the names given in ancient rituals as Jubelum Akirop, sometimes Abiram, Jubelo Romvel, and Jubela Gravelot. Schterke and Oterfilt are in some of the German rituals, while other Scottish rituals have Abiram, Romvel and Hobhen. For the Pérignan rite, we find Kunkel, Gravelot and Abyram Akirop which is the password, and in the catechism of the second elected official of Pérignan, "Romvel at the gate of the West, armed with a rule, Plover to that of the North, armed with a mallet and Abiram to

---

[46] < tinyurl.com/assassins-according-Mackey >.

that of the South, armed with a lever. It was he who knocked him to the ground and left him dead [47].

On the word ABIRAM, he writes: "One of the treacherous artisans, whose act of perfidy forms such an important part of the Third Degree, receives in some of the high ranks the name of Abiram Akirop. These words certainly have a Hebrew feel; but the significant words of Freemasonry have, in the lapse of time and in their transmission by ignorant teachers, become so corrupt in form that it is almost impossible to trace them to any intelligible root. They can be Hebrew or anagrammatized; but it is only chance that can give us the true meaning which the two words combined undoubtedly possess. The word Abiram means father of nobility, and may have been chosen as the name of the treacherous artisan with an allusion to the biblical story of Korah, Dathan and Abiram who conspired against Moses and Aaron. In the French ritual of the Second Chosen, it is said to mean murderer or assassin, but this does not appear to be etymologically correct. Brother Mackenzie suggests that Akirop may have come from Karab, Hebrew for joining the battle. He also proposes Abi-ramah, to mean "destroyer of the father" in Hebrew.

In its preliminary meaning, the loss of the Word signifying the death of Christ, the three murderers are the world, the flesh and the devil – to use the technical and conventional terms. The Master Builder who erected the House of Christian Doctrine is Christ himself. From another point of view, the evildoers were Pilate, Herod and Caiaphas . It is in this sense that *The Crowned Mason* replaces Judas, Caiaphas and Pilate, the three authors of the death of Jesus.

---

[47]Video, Assassins of the Third Degree: Encyclopedia of Freemasonry By Albert G. Mackey: <tinyurl.com/Mackey-assassins-les-Roses>.

Their names carry with them the villainy that makes them act. "Phanor, Amrou and Méthousaël had fled; but recognized as false brothers, they perished by the hands of the workers, in the states of Maacah, king of the land of Geth, where they hid themselves under the names of Sterkin, Oterfut and Hoben.

The Rosicrucians of Kilwinning named the three assassins Gain, Hakan and Heni.

Jean-Marie Ragon writes in *Philosophical and Interpretive Course of Ancient and Modern Initiations* : "we find the greatest confusion there; they are sometimes *Sterkin* or *Stolckin* , *Zéomet, Eléham* ; sometimes *Johaben* or *Johabert* , *Elechior, Tercy* ; sometimes *Toffet* (from *thopel* , ruina), *Tabaor* (*tebach* , occisio), *Edom* (*sanguineus*)" [48].

The Hebrew Bible calls them Akirof, Strakine and Astrafal [sic], while Islamic traditions call them Amrou, Phanor and Metoushaël [49].

The Templar sees there Squin de Florian, Noffo Dei Florentin and the Unknown on the testimony of whom Philip the Fair accused the order before the Pope, or even the three abominable ones, Philip the Fair, Clement V and Noffo Dei Florentin.
Picart, in a footnote to the *History of Religions and Morals of All Peoples of the World* (volume 6) suggests that " These three

---

[48] Jean-Marie Ragon, Philosophical and interpretative course of ancient and modern initiations, p.205: <tinyurl.com/assassins-selon-Ragon>.
[49] Dictionary of Gnostics and the main initiates from Wautier to the word Jubela, ...: <academia.edu/7042547>.

scoundrels represent for the Jesuits the three kingdoms which impolitely expelled them " [50].

At the York Rite, we know the names of the bad companions (Jubela, Jubelo, Jubelum) because they are missing, they are all three from Tyre. The companions expressly named are present on the site (Amos, Caleb, Ezra, Joshua, Hezekiah, Nathan, Samuel Isaiah, Aholiab, Gideon, Haggui, Daniel).

In English, Hiram's three assassins are collectively called the *Juwes*. Author Stephen Knight accused Freemasonry of being behind the Jack the Ripper murders because of the phrase found on a wall after the murder of Catherine Eddowes: " *The Juwes are the men that Will not be Blamed for nothing .*"

Albert Pike connects the name of the criminals to a triad of stars grouped in the constellation Lyra and draws attention to the fact that an ancient Chaldean god, Baal (*Beth, Lamed*), designated as an incarnation of the demon by the Jews, also appears in the three names Jubela, Jubelo, and Jubelum.

Gérard de Nerval, in *The Nights of Ramazan , chapter XII, Macbenach* recounts the testimony of a faithful companion of Adoniram to Solomon: I recognized that the first is a mason, because he said: I mixed the limestone to the brick, and the lime will crumble to dust. The second is a carpenter ; he said: I have extended the crosspieces of the beams, and the flame will visit them. As for the third, he works metals, these were his words: I took lavas of bitumen and sulfur from the poisoned lake of Gomorrah; I mixed them with the cast iron. At this moment, a shower of sparks lit up their faces. The mason is Syrian and his name is Phanor; the

---

[50] History of religions and morals of all the peoples of the world: <tinyurl.com/assassins-pour-les-jesuites>.

carpenter is Phoenician, he is called Amrou; the minor is a Jew from the tribe of Reuben, his name is Methusael [51].

They are named in a ritual of the Misraïm rite of 1820: Hakibouth (at the south gate), Hahemdath (at the west gate) and Haghebouroth (at the east gate), Hebrew names which mean pride, ambition and greed. .

The three bad companions who attack the master are the avatars of error symbolized by the reversal of the symbolism of the rule (image of truth), of fanaticism symbolized by the square (image of rectitude), of the authority of Mallet but authority that we try to usurp through pride.

The villains use tools, without knowledge of them, to kill the Master Builder. The first tool, the rule used without the compass by the felon, is the exalted imagination which pursues its own desires to infinity, outside of all reality. The second tool, the popular lever (or the square according to the rites, or the roller in the Luquet Ritual) becomes the instrument of tyranny in the hands of the multitude and expects, even more than the rule, the royalty of wisdom and virtue. The third lethal blow is given with the mallet, the tool of the Venerable! This refers to the duality of knowledge and nature. This aspect of the legend teaches us that altered or counterfeit knowledge is no longer used for construction but for destruction. "We will emancipate ourselves from mental slavery because while others might liberate the body, none but ourselves can liberate the mind. The mind is your only sovereign, sovereign. The man who is not able to develop and use his mind is necessarily the slave of the other man who uses his mind." (Marcus Garvey).

---

[51] Gérad de Nerval, *Voyage en Orient, Les nuits du Ramazan* , p.125: <tinyurl.com/les-nuits-du-Ramazan>.

For most of the rites which retain the moral aspect of the legend, Hiram's assassins are the vices which prevent one from achieving a state of perfection, the nine masters in search of Hiram's body are the virtues and duties Masonic. This interpretation is similar to the explanation given to the mirror rite: we would be our own worst enemy!

We should not dismiss the interpretation of Hiram's death as that of the solar cycle and then the three companions are the winter zodiac signs, those who give death to Hiram: Libra, Scorpio and Sagittarius who, towards the middle of autumn, occupy these three points of the sky, so that the first is towards the decline or to the west, the second on its right ascension to the south, and the last begins to appear to the east, this which is represented by the eastern gate where Hiram dies; as the sun dies in Sagittarius and is immediately reborn or begins a new year in Capricorn. The three assassins correspond to the three signs of autumn, which cause the death of the day star. The name Abi Balah (murderer of the father), which bears the most guilty, sufficiently designates Sagittarius, a constellation which in fact brings death to the sun, father of all things (*rerum omnium pater*).

With Jean Marie Ragon, this is the place to notice the perpetual effect of the equivocal meanings of most words in translations ; we will cite, for example, the two words kill and resurrect. To kill is translated from the Latin word *occider* e, from which we made occident, and this very common word does not represent to our mind neither murder, nor assassination, nor anything revolting, because the west, in allegorical style, is the 'to be, time, or the point in the world which kills, because it makes the sun disappear, and alternately all the stars; likewise, by a bold metamorphosis, we find the word *resurgere* , translated by the word to resuscitate, although this Latin verb never meant to return to life, but to rise a second time, to rise again, which is appropriate perfectly in the sun [52].

The story of Hiram's assassination by three evil companions aims to show a clear difference between good and evil, but is this separation really that clear?

Gérard de Nerval, in *Les nuits du Ramazan* [53], **explains their action, placing the blame on Hiram** because "He enslaved the carpenters to the miners. The second: He subordinated the masons to the miners. The third: He wanted to rule over the miners. "The first replied: He gives his strength to strangers. The second: He has no homeland. "The third adds: That's good. Companions are brothers ,... the first began again. Corporations have equal rights, continued the second. The third added: "It's good."

Using this type of motive, wouldn't the bad companions who kill the master be workers oppressed by a bad boss who refused any increase in wages ? Would they not be rebels against a heavy, unjust and closed order? Doesn't their fatal outburst reveal, in fact, the brutal cruelty of the patriarchal order embodied by the father [54]?
So should bad companions be condemned to death ? [55]

---

[52]Philosophical and interpretative course of ancient and modern initiations: <tinyurl.com/cours-philosophique>.

[53]Travels in the Orient, History of the Queen of the Morning and of Suleiman, Prince of Geniuses, Chap.V, The Sea of Brass: <tinyurl.com/la-mer-d-airain>.

[54] Video: Henri Laborit, *PRAISE of flight* : <tinyurl.com/inhibition-de-l-action>.

[55] *Plea for Three Bad Companions* : <ledifice.net/7077-C.html>.

The ambiguity between fault and innocence

The elevation ceremony features alternative **and ambiguous role plays** . At the REAA, the received companion is treated at the start of the reception as guilty and yet, we know him to be innocent since he will succeed the ideal master. During the epopty which narrates the murder, the recipient, although still a companion, plays the role of Hiram **;** he is both the one who transmits and the one who receives the example of respect for commitment until death, he is the disciple and the master.

Did Hiram himself not comply with the threats by revealing his secret since it is said that, if Solomon substituted words, it was because he thought that his Master builder had given in to pressure? of his attackers?

The last master received "resurrected" during the ceremony of receiving the rank of Master, takes the temporary place of Hiram's corpse to test the innocence of the recipient who must step over him.

The very respectable master and the two supervisors play the bad companions who participate in the assassination; apart from being at the same time the officers, all three of them intervene in the recovery of the dead. By causing the loss of speech, they will create substituted speech.

No role in life is definitive, it depends on social determinism and the nature of the problem facing the group.

The natural pooling of needs, security and strength can therefore be the moral meaning of a cooperative and peaceful organization of groups [56].

---

[56] Video, *experiment on rats by Didier Desore* : <tinyurl.com/Faits-comme-des-rats>.

The responsibility of the murderer

By choosing new apprentices among laymen, are the masters not introducing "bad Freemasons"? Could the scandals that are so popular among journalists have been avoided by more judicious selections?

Beyond this reality, there is above all the understanding that an act of treason can only be, all things considered, an **act serving the destiny of the murdered.**

Let's take the example of Judas, Jesus' companion. If for the Bible, the cause of Judas Iscariot is not defensible [57], others think that by delivering Jesus, Judas would have "forced" Jesus to fulfill his destiny and that without him Jesus would have fled. It is in this sense that Armand Abécassis suggests understanding the actions of Judas. Seeing that Jesus is not fully assuming his role as Messiah, and that the religious authorities are plotting against him, Judas wants to accelerate the course of events. He fervently believes that Jesus is the Messiah and wants the latter to confront the high priests so that they understand their error [58]. Still others give credence to the idea that it was Jesus himself who asked him to hand him over to the authorities so that he could be delivered from his material body and return to the light: "Do what you must do, do -THE"! Judas participated in God's plan by delivering Jesus; if he had not died on the cross, Christianity would probably never have been born.

---

[57] Is the cause of Judas Iscariot defensible? < tinyurl.com/la-cause-de-Judas >.

[58] Judas the most faithful of Jesus' disciples: <tinyurl.com/Judas-fidele-de-Jesus>.

Was not the role of Judas, apparently harmful, essential in the messiahship of Jesus?

Likewise, aren't the bad companions the hand of destiny to found the myth of Hiram? "Without them, there they are forever inside these demons, impossible to name them, therefore impossible to fight them and learn to master them. Without them our passions would forever reign over us, in the sleepiness of our conscience and the complacency of our ego. Without them there would be no murder. Without murder, no investigation, without investigation, no quest. Without our three companions the quest stops, or worse , it doesn't even begin. Without the murder of Hiram, there is no founding sacrifice of the myth. Without murder no lost word, without lost word no quest to find it, without quest no substitution, without substitution no rebirth, without rebirth no new Masters, without Masters no initiations, without initiations, no free Mason" [59].

In short, a way of putting Hiram's story in a Christlike vein !

The error of interpretation

We should not dismiss the interpretation of Hiram's death as that of the solar cycle and then the three companions are the winter zodiac signs, those who give death to Hiram: Libra, Scorpio and Sagittarius who, towards the middle of autumn, occupy these three points of the sky, so that the first is towards the decline or to the west, the second on its right ascension to the south, and the last begins to appear to the east, this which is represented by the eastern gate where Hiram dies; as the sun dies in Sagittarius and is immediately reborn or begins a new year in Capricorn. The three

---

[59] Plea for Three Bad Companions : <ledifice.net/7077-C.html>.

assassins correspond to the three signs of autumn, which cause the death of the day star. The name Abi Balah (murderer of the father), which bears the most guilty, sufficiently designates Sagittarius, a constellation which in fact brings death to the sun, father of all things (*rerum omnium pater*).

With Jean Marie Ragon [60], this is the place to notice the perpetual effect of the equivocal meanings of most words in translations; we will cite, for example, the two words kill and resurrect. To kill is translated from the Latin word *occider* e, from which we made occident, and this very common word does not represent to our mind neither murder, **nor assassination, nor anything revolting, because the west, in allegorical style, is the 'being, time, or the point in the world that kills, because it makes the sun disappear, and alternately all the stars** ; likewise, by a bold metamorphosis, we find the word *resurgere* , translated by the word to resuscitate, although this Latin verb never meant to return to life, but to rise a second time, to rise again, which is appropriate perfectly in the sun.

---

[60] Jean Marie Ragon, Philosophical *and interpretive course of ancient and modern initiations* , nbp. 1, p.161: <tinyurl.com/Mort-d-hiram-cycle-solaire>.

Lights towards the Middle Chamber

8 HIRAM'S LAST TEMPTATION

Poor fools! Will you be so naive as to believe that we are openly teaching you the greatest and most important secret? I assure you that anyone who wants to explain according to the ordinary and literal meaning of the words what the Hermetic philosophers write will find themselves caught in the twists and turns of a labyrinth from which they will not be able to escape.

Artéphuis

At that moment, when the daylight had just taken on the white color of midday, the man stood in the silence of the deserted construction site. The workers, exhausted by the heat and so many years of work, had returned to shady places. The temple was completed. It was flamboyant and the man, in solitude, looked at himself as in a mirror, face-to-face with the accomplished work, erected in the sweat and knowledge of its builders. It has already been ten years since the man left his country, the kingdom of Tyre, to come here, on this hill, at the request of King Solomon, to raise a sanctuary dedicated to the God of the Hebrews. The unusual silence indicated the completion of the work. The sacred space was finally demarcated. The man moved forward slowly and entered the narthex one last time. Between the two columns, which he had cast in brass to attest to the hierogamy of heaven and earth, he stopped, turned around, leaving the square of the Holy of Holies behind him, dominating the city that a pure ray of sunlight illuminated. Jerusalem seemed to belong to heaven.

His pain of being exiled was long gone. An indescribable peace inhabited him today. By participating in the creation of the temple, he entered into spiritual communion with the people of Israel. The work, by sanctifying a thought and its gestures, had allowed him to merge with the universe and in this cosmic reunification to find communion with light. This is one of the messages he wrote in his columns. The man decided, suddenly, in his meditation to go back and prepare for his return to Tyre. A desire to close a circle, to return to the initial point to recharge oneself in order to continue.

- Would it still be possible? Is the beginning always in the same place? Are time and my journey a circle or a spiral? Will they let me find what I left behind?

A youthful haste pushed him to quicken his steps. He went down towards one of the exits of the enclosure.

- Yes, I'm leaving. I'm going home. What I have completed here, I will rebuild elsewhere. Perhaps in Saba where new projects are opening and the message received from Egypt, inscribed here, will be revealed there too! Through the builders, the word must spread. Let's go!

With an energy revived by his plans, the man headed towards the nearest exit, at the Porte du Midi. His face glowed with the wisdom that for some, in middle age, reflects an active past during which experiences are internalized. The sensuality of his features showed his generosity, his firm and lively step, his determination. Tall and slender, her figure attested to a healthy life whose only excesses were those of thought. Despite his years, a great strength, which we guessed was unalterable, gave him this sovereign beauty, made of a delicate harmony where intelligence, gentleness, spirituality, righteousness mingle. The man's gaze commanded respect: It was that of a master, the Master Builder of the Temple and his name was Hiram Abi, which means Hiram the father. Suddenly a shadow appeared on the ground.

- He is certainly a worker, since only they have access to this place! But what can he do at this too ardent hour, why doesn't he rest like the others?

Concealed from the solar fire in the folds of his long woolen garment, a comp ø from the construction site placed himself between the southern exit and Hiram, as if to deny him access. In his hand the graduated ruler. Hiram recognized *Séterkin* , the maç ø also called *Phanor* , with the face of a lion.

- May peace be with you. Can I help you with anything ? Are you looking for something?

- We were a united group of comp ø but you chose a small number of us to distinguish them. However, we were all working together on the same work. Today, their heads are surrounded by a particular headgear which designates them as our masters. I know you gave them a password that gives them access to the power to rule. I don't want to wait any longer to also benefit from the mark of their superiority. Give me this password so that I too can use privileges.

- Child! What impudence, thought Hiram amused but disappointed by this vindictiveness, Too bad! A builder! He wants to do like so many others, out there, outside. He wants to dominate. He gave in to the temptation of identity in pride and self-importance. His impatience is a failure of the teaching given to him. The ardor is sometimes right but it takes infinite preparations, infinite precautions to lead the life of a man, the very creation of creation. No one can access knowledge that they do not even suspect. Otherwise it is to degrade the path of those who make the effort to advance on it. His vanity wants to rush the time of awakening and his quest is diverted. Has he not understood the symbolic indication of the rule he is holding? It is a graduation of the twelve hours of the day. An awareness of time. But without the compass he no longer has any adjustment to the measure, to the reasonably knowable. The rule without the compass is the exalted imagination which pursues its own desires to infinity , outside of all reality. His aspiration to power is a castrating ambition for the manifestation of the generous modalities of being. Wanting to take precedence over others is to deny the spirit of fraternity which is established in this community of builders. He still believes in a hierarchy of powers. It is only a degree of knowledge. It is duties that are the true sources of rights. It is in the difference in duties that the distinction of groups lies. Moreover…

With kindness, Hiram tried to explain to the comp ø his impossibility, moreover, of communicating the Master's message to him.
- I alone cannot grant you this favor.
The comp ø insists, paralyzed in his understanding by his ambition.
- Fool, that 's not how I received it, nor how he should ask himself. Work, persevere and you will be rewarded.
Séterkin, the mason loses his temper, threatens. The master remains calm but inflexible. Then the hand rises and strikes, aiming for the throat. But, deviated, the rule hits Hiram in the right shoulder on the collarbone, who, under the shock of surprise and the wave of this violence, staggers and puts his right knee to the ground.
- I don't want to confront him with force. Force cannot change a state of mind. Let's leave it!

Hiram gets up and walks away to avoid a fight. Concerned by this incident, in pain, he heads towards another exit at the western gate. But the companion was not alone. An accomplice was waiting in front of the second exit. Understanding his sidekick's failure, he immediately appears threatening, frozen like a goat ready to charge:

- You must give me the password. I am *Otefut* also called *Amron,* the carpenter. You are a bad boss. You have created hierarchies between your workers. The salary of M ø is higher than mine, I envy them. I am as educated as them, I want to get the same pay. Speak and pronounce the word of the Masters so that I receive my salary in the middle room.

Hiram understands that there is a conspiracy. However, a new worry does not discourage him. He explains firmly as he sees the lever in the man's hand.

- Since your name Amron means to speak, to reveal, know that speech without action is nothing. The discipline that you have granted to the community of carpenters does not accommodate either satisfied stupidity or vanity. It is absurd that those who intend to work with a square should care about prestige and personal favors. This means renouncing the very essence of builder solidarity. This is disobeying the norm. Your square tells you that you can only build on what is just, driven by the spirit of fairness. The lever you hold is your will which will prevail if it is based on absolute dedication to a high, noble and generous cause. To circumvent the rules, to be the smartest, more demanding, to want without deserving better pay, is to condemn the virtue of the order established between the different groups of workers. The secret that you ask for is in inner peace, in a response that you will make to yourself and which puts everything in its place and every man where he can support the building. Passion, ambition, vanity, unreason take you away from this path on which you were committed. No one can travel it for you and the Master's word is further along your path. Persevere, work, seek and you will find.

But Otéfut hears nothing, with a fanatical gesture he strikes with the lever which reaches the back of the Master's neck.
- A tool too!
The blow is dazzling, painful.
- Build, destroy with the same object! Sublimation and perversion present themselves in the same way. I was right. My columns do not deny it. Perverting the use of the lever removes all the fruits of teaching. This man has become profane again.

Hiram now seeks to escape what is closing in on him. These impatient and demanding comp ø have become the guardians of an opening closed forever. At the eastern gate , the final exit which avoids dragging his attackers towards the *kodech kodechim,* the Holy of Holies, the Master comes up against *Habirama* the minor, also called *Méthoushaël,* by his other name *Hoben.* The way of comp ø is shrill like that of a snake. Hiram instinctively measures all the hatred of man. Seeing the mallet he holds in his hand, he smiles despite the increase in his pain at the two points of impact of the tools.
- The symbol of the Master! Ah if he had wanted to direct his thoughts towards intelligence, perseverance, moral conscience, but his name, the one who kills the father, tells me very clearly what will happen.
Hiram has no doubt that the man will try to reach him with the tool transformed into a weapon. He is not scared. But he knows that the death of the spirit that he reads in the eyes of his attacker is his death:
- Give me the word from the Master! You can't escape anymore.
And without waiting, with his mace, Habirama strikes the Master on the forehead with a fatal blow. Thus the genius of darkness, which is in every being, had aroused the passions to try to ruin the work, by throwing trouble among the comp ø who already initiated into the first secrets of art

saw themselves as victims of injustice and partiality because they had not been recognized as Master.

- Not to fall, not to lose my balance, to still struggle to be, to refuse the threat, to no longer feel this paralysis which asphyxiates me, which puts my consciousness to sleep. I want to live upright. I created, protected, loved. All my gestures of living abandon me. How painful I am! I am so lonely. It would be enough to say and someone would help me, support me, perhaps treat me. Ah these torments of betrayal where everything is reversed and of the pain that I can no longer control. Companions , what have you done with your teaching? You do not know what you are doing. You have become a chimera with the head of a lion and a goat, and the tail of a serpent. My strength is leaving me, one word would be enough, my life for one word - - - Iod - Hé - Vav - Hé, Iod - Hé - Vav - Hé, 10, 5, 6, 5… The letters follow one another and turn before his eyes.

- Password, Master's word, key word to open but also to close, for the passage from my life to death. All the knowledge of esoteric doctrine is contained in these 4 letters. To name is to create, but to pronounce the word alone is to say nothing. And yet, I must live. I am the custodian of a part of the word which will disappear if each of the custodians does not transmit their piece of the key. This word is only complete if united with King Solomon and the King of Tyre, we pronounce together what is unpronounceable, alone.

At that time, a king was an initiate to the higher plane who was wearing a crown or tiara and who was capable of teaching following the initiatory path, the royal way. The king of Tire owned all the materials of wood and metal. *There is strength in him!* The king of Israel designed and transformed for the construction of the temple. *In him the foundation!* Hiram, sent from Tire to King Solomon, by carrying out the work closes the triangle in an inseparable synthesis of *having-acting-being* .

- No one knows my secret. As a Master I still have to teach another Master so that he replaces me and so that the chain does not break. I must live! But how can you live without telling someone who cannot understand. I only know the letters in their form, not the phoneme. The tetragrammaton is not pronounced. No challenge to overcome, no heroic determination. Either way, they can't understand. So why not give in? Say it to myself at least once. Make the torment stop. Gather my strength and say to survive.
He tried to breathe: *AUMMM* ....
- Say, go ahead, speak, give me the word, insisted the felon.

Hiram closes his eyes.
- Say and let them believe that the word is enough. No ! It is the evil in my flesh that capsizes my thoughts. Evil must be silenced . I have testified for knowledge by my life, my work and my wisdom. My death must also bear witness. Should secrecy be preserved at the cost of life ? Is the secret worth it in itself? Or rather by the way we experience it? My death will guarantee the secret, even if it erases it. I searched for the answer that would end my questioning. This response can only be heard from me. It's not that of the other, it's the one that I make mine. It's my faith. I will not betray her by letting this companion believe anything else. I am , even if he has renounced being. Without this challenge with the unbearable, I would never have known the hope that one must have. My life was like a busy day and now I can be tired. The law of man is not possession, it is expectation. To say this would not only be betraying myself but also betraying the teaching given to my murderers. I'm dying. But try, at least once, to pronounce the ineffable alone. To

attempt a final sound integrating all the parts into unity, perhaps finally found.

A cloud veiled the sun. As he collapsed, Hiram murmured a word that Habirama did not hear. She lost herself in death. Had he pronounced this word from M ø or was his last breath to say " *vanity of vanities*" or " *buttom of rose* " or any other word of a now impossible dream. When Hiram died he entered the light and speech was lost.
Upon learning of Hiram's death, Solomon was obliged to replace the lost words with a substitute word: the first words spoken by the MM ø who discovered the dead man's body once again sealed the secret of mastery; This is what Masonic rituals tell us.

So! "Invent, frantically invent, without worrying about connections, until you can no longer make a summary. A simple relay game, between emblems, one which speaks for the other, without pause. Break the world down into a saraband of chain anagrams, and then believe in the inexpressible [61]." Is this not the true reading of the Torah?
But we ask ourselves questions.
How is it that, knowing that the word could only be through the meeting of the 3 (King Solomon, the king of Tire and Hiram), how is it that none of them thought of pass on your own knowledge to a disciple so that the chain does not break if you disappear? Was it believing oneself to be immortal?
It seems that Master's new word is shared by more than three Masters. In the ritual of the Ancient Accepted Scottish Rite , all those who witness the elevation of the body are witnesses to the secret word (the Grand Expert , the 3 Masters who guard the corpse , the 2nd [Warden], the [1st] Warden

---

[61] Umberto Eco, Foucault's Pendulum.

eillant , 7 Masters who delimit the middle room. This means that all the Masters have access to this word! There was therefore previously an implicit hierarchy due to secrecy. Is the one who directs the work more than a Master ? For us, there is nothing above the Master.

So what could it mean that only 3 had access to secret knowledge? Considering that among the Hebrews, the high priest, the *Cohen Gadol,* was the only holder of the orthoptic and total pronunciation of the sacred word that he vocalized once a year in the Holy of Holies, this could mean that the word was not lost and that if Solomon replaced it, it was because he thought that his Master Builder had given in to the pressure of his attackers.

So by moving from one plane of analysis (the real) to another (the symbolic) and by confusing them in reasoning, we end up saying almost everything we want and even its opposite. In any case, it is this type of question that arises when reading the legend of Hiram that we have revisited. There are several temptations of Hiram evoked by our work:

- That of returning to your country to pursue a work. She is desire.

- The one that we have only touched on, but not retained, is that of speaking to give in to the threat of comp ø

- Finally two final temptations seem interesting: that of speaking to survive and save the secret which is in a symbolic triangulation of the two kings of Israel and Tire and Hiram which is the synthesis of dualisms.

- That of pronouncing, all by himself, the forbidden word. It is both a sin of pride, perhaps, but above all a metaphysical curiosity to resonate on a cosmic level with the name of the Ineffable.

Hiram, a mythical character, embodies for Freemasonry a syncretism of these beings who must die to resurrect , to found a current of Tradition. This Hiram could not have had the ultimate temptation to pronounce, alone, the unpronounceable. This was only a psychological artifice to question us, because Hiram, as an initiate, knows the abomination that would be the literal understanding of mythical fiction. All the terms designating the mystery, the spirit, the being, the substance, the One, the essence, the alpha and the omega, are words objectifying or personifying. Only the mystery immanent in existence, the harmonious organization of the universe and human emotion in the face of this mysterious aspect in which everything that really exists (beings and things) participates. The name "God", if it is not misused, means absolutely nothing other than emotion in the face of the inexplicable [62].

The creator and judge of monotheism (iod, hey, vav, hey) are united in a single symbol, the meaning of which is the mystery of existence, in which the mystery of human life is included. Consequently the name "God" implies responsibility for the choice between good and evil, which is attested by the Tables of the Mosaic Law. To name is to bring into existence. Latin _ *exsistere* , to exist is understood as "to come out of, to rise from". Existence is therefore imagined as an exit from infinite harmony. The expulsion, which is to say the emanation to which the root of the term "to exist" alludes, is not necessarily a reality, but an image joining the personifying image of the myths, of the symbol of the creator. For us, it is not explanatory. Solomon says: " the image strives to express the immeasurable. Jerusalem (Hebrew culture) will be destroyed, like all culture, when the

---

[62] See the chapter *The word that cannot be spoken: the Tetragram* of the Booklet *Luminescence of words and silences* from the Masonic Vagabondages Collection.

abomination settles in the Temple, when the name of God is taken for the living name. The abomination would be to use the name without reference to the mysteries. What vanity could be greater than the pretension of a metaphysical speculation which not only would like to pronounce the name God, but which, ignoring the symbolic meaning, would affirm by pronouncing it the confusion between the symbol and the mystery called God?

The initiation teaching centers called Mysteries existing in Egypt, in Greece, and among all peoples of high culture, had the aim of awakening emotion before the mystery of universal harmony, to which man, for its essential good, must be incorporated by way of self-harmonization; from which follows the living feeling of immanent ethics, true religiosity. Hiram, an initiate, knows that this cannot be said, not because it is forbidden, but because it is impossible.

Today, the temptation of certain Freemasons is to believe they know how to pronounce the names Liberty, Equality, Fraternity, Tolerance and to be content with these incantatory murmurs, thinking that this is enough to make them exist.

9 STORIES LIKE HIRAM'S

The object of Masonic legends is not to establish historical facts but to convey philosophical doctrines.

The geographical area of Masonry is, roughly, the world of the Bible, or what is still called "the world known to the Ancients", in short the Mediterranean basin, with more or less advanced extensions, to the north, in the European continent. The traditions to which Masonry is "united by multiple links" are therefore, among the living traditions, Judaism, Christianity and Islam, and, among the less widespread traditions, the Egyptian, Greco-Latin and Celtic traditions. It is therefore there that we find stories which tell of the fundamental unity and identity of traditions which all have not failed to raise the question of violence, murder and the recovery of the murdered. It is through myth that the experience of dying and coming back to life, of being on the verge of death and coming back, is truly experienced .

The epopty of Hiram presented to the Freemasons, from the 3rd ^{degree} **, also raises the question of violence, murder and the recovery of the murdered. This is why I** suggest you explore some tales, legends and myths which in their story clearly show analogies with that of Hiram.

THE TALE (or fable) is a narration that is transmitted over time through orality. It was born from the

progressive forgetting of the religious character of the story.

The tale appears as the mirror of man, revealing his faults and his hatreds, but also making known the strength of his ideals. For Bruno Bettelheim "This is exactly the message that fairy tales, in a thousand different ways, deliver to the child: that the struggle against the serious difficulties of life is inevitable and an intrinsic part of human existence, but that if , instead of shying away, we firmly face the expected and often unfair trials, we overcome all obstacles and we end up achieving victory.

The tale is a short story belonging to the world of poetry. Before the 19th century, it was part of the register of the marvelous, then that of the fantastic.

Everything that is fabulous or terrifying settings, fairies, magic, dragons, genies and elves, constitute these tales which seduce the imagination, without worrying more than is necessary, foreseeing a happy ending. The tale sometimes takes us to fabulous lands where time does not exist.

Alice's Tale in Wonderland

Written in 1865 by Charles Lutwidge Dodgson, under the assumed name of Lewis Caroll (Freemason?), the tale *of Alice in Wonderland* is a surrealist text whose analysis can be appreciated thanks to the author's illustrations .

This tale can also be interpreted as a series of events related to Masonic initiation, revealing the inner journey of the Initiate. A pleasant hermeneutical suggestion can be viewed as a continuation of the previous video.

Snow White's Tale

Snow White appears to be initiated by carrying out the journeys symbolized first by the flight through the forest considered as a descent into hell, then by work, such as housekeeping, in the house of the dwarves, then by the death to which she escapes thanks to the kindness of soul of the hunter, finally by resurrection in the form of waking up surrounded by animals in a reassuring climate lulled by light and tranquility.

During her meeting with the seven (7) dwarves, Snow White personifies the domination of the spiritual soul over the faculties of the individual soul represented by them.

The heroine reaches a spiritual level with her second initiatory death, during her poisoning by the queen. The queen, who now appears in the guise of a witch, embodies the infernal possibilities of the human being, then taking on a satanic dimension to disappear, however, into nothingness (falling into the ravine, illusory symbol of such possibilities) pushed by the dwarves (symbols of the faculties of the human soul capable of destroying evil).

Working in the mines, the 7 dwarves were often seen as an alchemical representation of the 7 metals: seven metals (gold, silver, tin, copper, iron, lead, mercury) lead, tin , iron mercury, copper, silver, gold.

Snow White will have first reached the death of the profane state, through her flight into the forest and, secondly, the death of individuality by biting the apple. She will be reborn under the kiss of the divine rider, illuminated by the rays of the star of light. As for the dwarves, who have become symbols of the powers of the soul, they remain alone, in a parallel world, out of reach.

The vain, jealous and destructive queen is forced to put on fire-reddened pumps and dance with them until she dies.

The tale symbolically says that if our passions are not curbed and controlled, they end up destroying us.

Like many tales, Snow White shows that to change is to have to give up something that you have previously enjoyed, at the cost of difficult and painful experiences that cannot be avoided.

THE LEGEND , from the Latin *legenda,* is what must be read. It is this meaning of the word legend which corresponds to an explanation, a comment added to a drawing, a plan. Popularly the word "legend" has become a traditional story where reality is distorted and embellished,
Unlike tales which take place in the world of the imagination, legends have a plausible character and tell the story of events which took place or which could have taken place.
The legend contains elements of the marvelous and is based in certain cases on historical facts which have been transformed by beliefs, or by popular imagination, or by poetic invention.
The form of the legend is simple and its essential object is the miracle.
Originally, the legend recounted the lives of the saints. Nowadays, they are wonderful accounts of a past event based on an authentic tradition but often modified over time. Unlike myth, legend is not based on deities.

We find only two fables in the entire Bible : that of the trees choosing a king (Judg 9:8,15) and that of the thorn and the cedar (2Ki 14:9). But there are many legends contained in what is known as the *Hagada.* "Ezra, his disciples and their successors, who are called "Sopherim" (men of the Book, commentators on the Law), proceeded to re-educate the people [the Judeans returning from exile in Babylon] in means of public readings of the Bible translated into Aramaic and accompanied by explanations, comments and paraphrases. This reading of the law took place every week, on holidays, Saturdays and market days, so that the "people of the countryside could, by going there, benefit from this teaching. At the same time as it was being explained, sermons were given on the biblical text (homilies), and it was illustrated with anecdotes and parables, many of which have been preserved [63].

The Legend of Master Jacques

The Companionship of Devoir (or Saint-Devoir de Dieu as it is sometimes called) claims to have been created by a fabulous character named Maître Jacques.

In the ancient tradition of the Companions passers of the fraternity known as the "children of Master Jacques", and among the current Companions passers of duties, Jacques is a Pyrenean originally from Carte. He was commissioned by Hiram of Tyre, on behalf of King Solomon, to build the Temple in Jerusalem around 900 BC. He is a gander, a master stonemason, initiated into the nature of stone and legend notes that he has been cutting stone since the age of fifteen. This same legend gives Maître Jacques as responsible for the Jachin column and perhaps also for the Boaz column of the first Temple in Jerusalem. For Perdiguier, he built two dodecagon columns, the Vedrera column and the Macaloe column. On these columns were carved various scenes from the Old Testament : the fall of Adam and Eve, David's dream as well as episodes from the life of Master James himself.

Some legends say that, once the Temple was completed, James left Judea in the company of another master, Soubise, with whom he soon fell out and from whom he separated. The ship carrying Soubise landed in Bordeaux. James landed in Marseille with his thirteen companions and his forty disciples. He traveled for three more years, during which he had to defend himself against the ambushes of the disciples of Soubise who one day attacked him and threw him into a

---

[63] The formation of marriage in biblical and Talmudic law: <tinyurl.com/Droit-biblique>.

swamp; he managed to hide behind some rushes. His disciples came and helped him. Finally Jacques retired to Provence in the hermitage of Sainte-Baume. The story of his end seems to have been modeled on the story of the Passion of Christ. One of his disciples, the infamous Jeron (also called Never), betrayed him. One morning, while he was praying in a remote place, Jeron came to him, gave him the kiss of peace, it was the agreed signal. Five assassins threw themselves at Maître Jacques and pierced him with five dagger blows. However, he lived for a few more hours and was able, before dying, to say goodbye to his late companions. When he was dying, he gave the kiss of peace to his brothers and recommended that they give it to future initiates so that the tradition would not be interrupted: "if they are faithful to their Duty, I will protect them."

Master Jacques, assimilated to Osiris, was symbolically cut into pieces, his hat went to the hatters, his tunic to the tailors, his coat to the carpenters, his belt to the carpenters, his staff to the wheelwrights and his sandals to the locksmiths. What was dispersed was what it represented: all the trades.

There Legend of Melchizedek

Enoch, after visiting creation and talking with God, returned to his family to settle his affairs and transmit the books he wrote to his people. God gave him 30 days before calling him back. After much advice, precepts and exhortations, Enoch having left, it was Methuselah who became priest and replaced his father Enoch. When Methuselah died (yes, yes, ...), it was Nir who became a priest.

The latter had a wife, Sophonim. She, too old to give birth, abandoned by her priest husband since he was designated as a priest by God, was nevertheless pregnant. Nir eventually discovered it, exchanged a few words with his wife, whom he accused, of course, of infidelity. She explained to him that she knew nothing about his condition. She ends up falling at Nir's feet, dead. Nir, greatly disturbed – we can understand this – called his brother Noah. He reassuringly offered to help Nir dig a grave in secret for his deceased wife and, above all, her pregnancy which was coming to term. The two men laid Sophonim on a bed, dressed him in black and went off to dig a grave.

Now, back in the room where they had left Sophonim's body, they discovered a young child. The latter, having just been born, sat, spoke and praised God. The two men washed and dressed the child in priestly (priest) clothing. They changed Sophonim to clothe her in more beautiful garments, and built another more glorious tomb for her and me anonymous. Finally, they named the child Melchizedek. And Noah said to his brother: "Keep the child in secret until the right time, because the people have become wicked in all the earth, and in some way; when they see him, they will put him to death . "

Nir thus took care of Melchisedech. Now, time had passed, the destruction promised by God being inevitable, Nir asked God to save the child from the massacre to come. God – who was much more talkative in those ancient times than he is today – answered him :

" […] but for the child do not worry, Nir, because I, in a short time, will send my archstrategist Michael, and he will take the child and place him in the garden of Eden […] and he will be my priest of priests, and I will sanctify him; and I will change him into a great people who will sanctify me."

Nir blesses god – and the precision on the birth that he gives does not lack spice: "[…] because your word has given a high priest in the womb of Sophonim my wife. For I have no descendants and this child will be my descendant, he will become like my son, and you will number him among your servants [….] and Melchisedech will be the head of the priests in another race.

Forty days after this exchange, the Angel Michael was sent, as planned, to retrieve the child. At first, Nir did not recognize him, refused to hand him over, fearing that the child would be killed by the "evil people" [64].

The **Legend of Renaud de Montauban**

The legend of the master builder Renaud de Montauban, builder of Cologne Cathedral, is very close to the myth of Osiris. Betrayed and murdered by workers, he was thrown into the river. The fish gathered to take his body out of the waters, body illuminated by three candles. Another legend says that it was a woman, an allusion to Osiris, who discovered the body. In the *Third Book* , Rabelais evokes the legend of Renaud de Montauban who allegedly killed a nephew of Charlemagne. A famous miniature, built like a chessboard, shows "how Renaut occited Berthoulet, the nephew of Charlemagne, by playing chess". Then he would have taken refuge on the construction site of the future Strasbourg cathedral. He would have behaved like an excellent worker but, a victim of the jealousy of his colleagues, would have been assassinated. This theme will be taken up in 18th century Masonry with the allusion to the murder of Hiram, Solomon's chief architect.

The legend of Oedipus

Parricide, unlike fratricide, makes room for the disappearance of an overarching hierarchy. This hierarchy or authority is an underrepresentation of the divine. Hiram is an artifex, just as Hiram of Tire is Rex and Solomon is Rex-Pontifex.

In Greek mythology, Oedipus was the son of Laios and Jocasta. To escape Apollo's prediction that he would be

---

[64] Summary written by La Masone from the text of the *Book of the Secrets of Enoch, Miraculous Birth of Melchisedech* , page 21: <tinyurl.com/Secrets-d-Henoch>.

killed by his own son, Laius ordered a servant to abandon the child on Mount Cithaeron, with both his feet nailed, to be devoured by wild beasts. But, instead, the servant entrusted him to a shepherd who later gave him to the Corinthian king Polybius and his wife Merope, without issue. They named him Oedipus (*Oidipous* meaning swollen feet) and raised him as their son. Oedipus grows up and rumors suggest that he is not his parents' son. He urges Mérope to tell him the truth, but the latter's answers are enigmatic. He then consults the Pythia of Delphi (his trip to Delphi, which he undertook alone, was intended to allow him to hear the oracle of Apollo, the god of Light and Truth) who predicted, without lifting the secret of his origins, that he will kill his father and marry his mother.

His journey then took him near Mount Cithaeron where he had been exposed to death when he was a child. This harmful place actually represents the re-enactment of what had happened years before, in this precise place, in circumstances which were engraved in his memory in an indelible way . Remembering the fatal curse of the prophetess, Oedipus hears the death sentence pronounced by his father. Oedipus felt dizzy, which confirms the emergence of early trauma. As he left the temple, he relived the dissociation of emotions generated by the brutal act, which is why it seemed to him that his heart was turning to stone. At the crossroads, an arrogant and vindictive old man who finds himself in front of Oedipus is none other than Laius, his executioner, surrounded by his henchmen. The son is now a warrior driven by the energy of his long-repressed rage. He can relive the extreme violence inflicted on him by these same protagonists and finally resolve the very origin of his neurosis. When his father raises his hand, he escapes death by knocking him out and killing his bodyguards. His fatal outburst reveals, in fact, the brutal cruelty of the patriarchal order embodied by the father.

Like Freud, who thought of Oedipus based on that of Sophocles, the Japanese psychiatrist Kosawa approached the Ajase complex based on a myth taken from a story by the Buddhist monk Shinran who lived in the 12th century. There we find ambivalence, murder, destiny and a notion known as "prenatal grudges".

Using this type of motive alleged in these legends, wouldn't the bad companions who kill the master be workers oppressed by a bad boss who refused any increase in salary? Would they not be rebels against a heavy, unjust and closed order? Aren't the rites of restructuring and purification the result of a feeling of guilt, or even an obsessive psychosis?

The legend of the Four Crowned

These saints were four brothers whose names were long unknown. They were called the *Four Crowned* because they received the palm of martyrdom and were crowned in Heaven in 304. Their apology is found, among other things, in the *Régius Manuscript* of 1390 (at the fifteenth point) [65].

They are often confused with the saints Claudius, Nicostratus, Symphorian and Castorius (and Simplice whom they converted) who were the marvelous sculptors of Rome and who were condemned, by Diocletian, to torture for having refused to sculpt the image of the god Aesculapius , considering that it was an idol. The lead coffins, where they were locked while still alive, were found by a certain Nicomedes who buried their remains at his home. Two years later, having built a temple dedicated to the cult of Aesculapius, Diocletian ordered his legionaries to pay homage to the god of medicine. Four soldiers, also converted to Christianity, refuse to participate in the sacrifices. They are arrested and beaten to death . Their names would only be known later: Second, S é v é rien,

---

[65] < tinyurl.com/Manuscrit-Regius >.

Carpophore and Victorien. In the meantime, sculptors and soldiers will have been registered with the Christian martyrologist under the name of the Four Crowned (Guy Chassagnard).

As a result of this confusion, the former became the patrons of builders and statuaries and, in general, of masons, sculptors, stonecutters. Their attributes are often given as a mallet, a square, a ruler or even a crown on their head as we see among the illuminations of the *Breviary of Isabella of Castile* [66]Throughout Europe the activities of architects, stone cutters and masons were under the protection of the four Crowned Saints.

Here is how the *Legenda Aurea* (13th century) by Jacopo da Varagine describes the hagiographical story of the Four Crowned: "The four crowned were Severus, Severinus, Carpophorus and Victorinus who, by order of Diocletian, were whipped with 'scourged with lead until they died. At first their names were unknown, but a long time later God revealed them. It was therefore decided that their memory would be honored under the names of five other martyrs, Claudius, Castorius, Symphorian, Nicostratus and Simplician, who suffered two years after them.

Now, these last martyrs were skillful sculptors who, having refused Diocletian to sculpt an idol, and to sacrifice to the gods, were put alive, by order of this emperor, in lead boxes and thrown into the sea around the year of the Lord 287. Pope Melchiades ordered to honor under the names of these five martyrs the four previous ones whom he called the four crowned, before their names were discovered; and the usage always prevailed, even when we knew what they were really called."

---

[66] *Breviary of Isabella of Castile* , 1490, pf484v: <tinyurl.com/breviaire-Isabelle-de-Castille>.

Only France has not adopted this patronage for building trades, having chosen Saint Thomas as its patron.

The first Masonic Lodge to have devoted its work to Masonological research, bears the name of *Quartet Coronati Lodge* n°2076 ; it was founded in 1884, under the auspices of the United Grand Lodge of England.

THE MYTH comes from the Greek muthos, story, fable or word. It is an anonymous and collective story which fulfills a socio-religious function. It most often serves as an element of cohesion between individuals in a group. The myth features characters who are most often superhuman and who have supernatural powers but with human behavior and feelings. The myth is a word, a fable which refers to ancient events full of meaning. In primitive societies, it serves as an explanation of the world, reporting how things began and why people are where they are today. It is considered absolutely true and recited in very specific circumstances, which distinguishes it from fables, tales and all invented stories. In its composition, it is most often very short and perfectly arranged. Every detail is charged with intense meaning.

Industrial societies have relegated myths to the domain of poetry and imagination. However, they remain the expression of a culture, they express the deep aspirations of the human unconscious and depict eternal situations. Scientific thought has not succeeded in making myths disappear despite the tension between the promises of meaning of the metaphysical potential of myths (muthos) and the demand for their validation in a rational and coherent discourse (logos).

We distinguish between myths which tell of the birth of the gods (theogony), those which explain the origin of the world (cosmogony), those which explore the fate of man after death (eschatology) and others, such as the myths of birth and rebirth (eternal return), the myths of the civilizing or cultural hero (Prometheus) or the myths of foundation (foundation of Rome by Romulus and Remus). The first three categories have close relationships with religions; many religious rites, in fact, reproduce certain aspects or certain details of the myths. Myths which do not fall into the above categories are the subject of folkloric stories, of elaborate poetic songs, which are found among the most diverse peoples, such as those transmitted by the bards in ancient Greece or those which continue to be transmit African griots today. Myths and legends have been transmitted to us in the writings of several ancient authors who remain with us. Homer and his *Iliad and Odyssey* , Hesiod in his *Theogony* , Ovid in his *Metamorphoses* ...

In societies where myths are still alive, the natives carefully distinguish : myths "true stories" from fables or tales "false stories". The Ancients considered as true stories all those which relate to the origins of the world, that is to say all those which deal with the sacred or the supernatural. In false stories, on the other hand, the subject is profane. This is the reason why myths cannot be told indifferently. In certain traditions they can only be told in front of initiates. Generally, old instructors communicate the myths to neophytes during their period of isolation, this being part of their initiation.

The myth of Osiris

One of the most complete narrations of the myth of Osiris is that of Plutarch, in his *De Iside et Osiride,* of which he had, we do not know how, a more complete knowledge than any Egyptian source, including that of the *Pyramid Texts* . Other possible sources are: the *Book of the Dead* , the texts of a stele found in the Louvre, other various texts from ancient Egypt, the research of specialists in ancient Egypt.

Lights towards the Middle Chamber

As he returns victorious from a long campaign of conquests, Seth takes advantage of the celebrations organized on this occasion to invite his brother Osiris to a banquet. During the evening, he challenges him to lie down in a large chest. When the latter was lying there, Seth locked him up and threw the chest into the Nile.

Isis, the Sister-Wife of Osiris, goes in search of his soul in order to bring him back to life. Isis tears her clothes and travels the world in search of the chest in which "the Benevolent" has been locked. However, when she returns, she will not bring back Osiris because those who go down to these places cannot return and it is only the love of Isis, symbol of regeneration and eternal life that will allow the body to be found. During Isis's journey to the underworld, the chest containing the body, carried by the sea, reached the coasts of Phoenicia where it washed up at the feet of an acacia tree, or a tamarisk tree, depending on the version. The quest lasted so long that the trunk of the acacia tree covered the box containing the body of Osiris.

The king of Byblos, busy building his new palace, had the tree cut down in order to make it one of the two columns which were to decorate the entrance. Isis hears about the smell that came from the trunk while it was being cut. She immediately understands its meaning and goes to Phoenicia where she is given the prodigious column. She opens the wooden column and removes her husband's coffin, which she waters with her tears. She takes him back to Egypt and hides him deep in the swamps so that Seth will not know that the body has been found. But during a hunt, the latter discovers the chest. Furious that Osiris is still whole despite the passage of time, he decides to cut the corpse into fourteen pieces which he scatters across the country. The number of pieces of Osiris' body varies according to sources, from fourteen to forty-two. Both versions of the Jumilhac Papyrus mention fourteen pieces collected by Isis in twelve days, which corresponds to the duration of the plowing festival. According to Diodorus Sicily, Typhon (another name for Seth, brother of Osiris, principle of evil, darkness and sterility) cut the body of his victim into twenty-six pieces, one for each conspirator. Each was given a mummiform appearance before being buried. Finally, the sacred geography of Edfu mentions as many pieces as nomes (administrative districts of Ancient Egypt), or forty-two. The dismembered body of Osiris, whose flood restores unity, thus merges with the land of Egypt. Here, the fourteen pieces represent those which are removed from the moon, in the waning phase, until its total disappearance. The quest for Isis and the reconstitution of the body illustrate, on the contrary, the ascending phase, until the reappearance of the full moon, reconstituted, the oudjat eye. Isis starts looking for the pieces. She finds them all except the penis, devoured by an oxyrhincus (or a Nile pike). Helped by Anubis, Thoth and Nephthys, she recomposes the dismantled body into twelve parts and mummifies it. Brought back to life by these practices and now safe from death, Osiris retreats into the underworld, he then leaves the throne of the visible world to his son Horus who will become the model of kings to come.

It is on the 17th ^{day} of the month of Athyr that Egyptian mythology places the death of Osiris: this is the time when the full moon is especially visible. So the Pythagoreans call this day "interposition", and they have a complete repugnance for the number 17. Indeed, between the square sixteen (4×4) and the rectangle eighteen (6×3), which are the only numbers of plane surfaces whose perimeters are equal to their areas, falls the number seventeen which disjoins these two numbers, interposes between them and divides their ratio into two unequal parts.

Thus, taken out of his acacia gangue, dismembered and recomposed, with the help of three other deities, Osiris will be raised and mummified (the papyrus of the *Book of the Dead* of Ani, discovered in Thebes in 1887 by Wallis Budge includes an invocation very special: *Homage to you, oh lord of Acacia). It is only at the end of this restructuring and this preparation for eternity that Osiris will be able to resume his journey. His bones are of silver, his flesh of gold, his hair of lapis lazuli* .

Plato, Thales, Eudoxus, Apollonius and Pythagoras had brought back from Egypt this principle, true or false, that in the economy of the universe life emerges from the bosom of death; this principle was presented under the allegory of Osiris expiring to be reborn under the name Horus.

The 3rd grade was called "death's door" in Egypt. The coffin of Osiris, whose assassination was supposed to have been recent, stood in the middle of the site where the ceremony took place. The aspirant was asked if he had taken part in the murder of Osiris. He was hit, or they pretended to be hit, on the head with an ax, he was knocked down, covered with mummy strips, lightning flashed, the supposed dead was surrounded by fire then brought back to life [67].

Assimilated to Dionysus, Osiris illustrated neo-Orphic theology: cosmogony conceived as a self-sacrifice of the divinity, as the dispersion of the One in the Multiple, followed by the "resurrection", that is to say by the gathering of the Multiple in the primordial Unity. This is how G. Mackey evokes the rapprochement of the Mysteries of Osiris with those of Freemasonry [68].

Osiris was very early compared to the buried (dying) grain of wheat, germinating and reappearing in the sunlight, ready to be the essential food of men. Many illustrations depict the god's mummy covered in grains of wheat, or young stalks of wheat emanating from his elongated body. Because

---

[67] J.M. Ragon, *Masonic Orthodoxy* , 1853, p. 101:
<tinyurl.com/Orthodxie-Maconnique

[68] Video, Mackey: <tinyurl.com/symbolisme-de-la-FM>.

he was the image of the cycles of nature, forms of Osiris were dug into the stone which were filled with earth, and in which grains of wheat were scattered so that it would grow in the secret of the tomb. Thus, buried at the same time as the deceased, wheat, the vital symbol of Osiris, was for the deceased the certainty of his future rebirth, the assurance of the continuity of his life, then of his luminous resurrection. Therefore, in the funerary papyrus of Nu, Osiris declares: "I am the Lord of men who will rise from the dead." It is such a symbolic image that Christ will use when he compares himself to the grain of wheat which must die in order to be reborn and produce new grains a hundredfold. Some Gnostics used this word to affirm that Christ had followed the entire Osirian initiatory journey in order to in turn become a spiritual Osiris, a being of Light.

The initiate of the 3rd grade of the mysteries of Isis was first led into a vestibule above the entrance to which was written "door of death". Mummies and coffins were depicted on the walls. He soon found a corpse. In the middle of the vestibule was placed the coffin of Osiris, which, because of his presumed assassination, was stained with blood. The aspirant was asked if he had participated in this murder; following this preparatory test, he passed into a room, where all the initiates were dressed in black; he was presented with a crown which he trampled under his feet, and the head of the initiation cried out "insult, vengeance!", and immediately grabbed the sacrificial ax and gently struck the candidate on the head. Instantly two initiates knocked him down and wrapped him in bandages; all those around him were in sadness; he was presented in this state of apparent death before a tribunal which declared that he had not participated in the murder of Osiris, and he was given freedom;…; the sign of recognition consisted of a special embrace [69].

Alexandre Lenoir with the *Explanation of an Egyptian papyrus* completes the connection that we make between the murders of Osiris and Hiram [70].

In alchemy, in the 17th century, the myth of Osiris was taken up by Michael Maier in his *Fugitive Atalante* which made it a fugue, an engraving and a poem on the themes of transformation, regeneration and rebirth [71].

In Greece, Osiris' counterpart is Dionysus-Zagreus. Born from an illegitimate union of Zeus, the child Dionysus incurs the hatred of Hera, who has him murdered and torn to pieces by the Titans; but another divinity, Apollo or Athena, brings together the tortured members, and the young god comes back to life; the biography of Atys, consort of Cybele, also includes castration, death and rebirth. We would never stop listing the gods whose history conforms to this itinerary, in which that of Hiram also fits.

The implementation of the myth of Hiram Abif, in the Egyptian rites of Freemasonry, is an operation of operational magic intended to make all master masons relive what the Egyptian priest-initiates ritualized in the great pyramid in order to transfer the spirit of the deceased pharaoh (Osiris) to the new designated pharaoh to make him a new Horus.

---

[69] Doctor Pierre Gérard Vassal , Complete Course of Masonry or General History of Initiation from its origin to its institution in France, 1832, p.244 and 245: <tinyurl.com/Cours-de-Franc-maonnerie>.

[70] Alexandre Lenoir: <tinyurl.com/Osiris-et-Hiram>.

[71] Patrick Burensteinas, stage 2, *The Alchemical Journey*, Chartres , video from 20'): <tinyurl.com/Burensteinas-Chartres>.

The primitive Egyptian religion, probably of Atlantean origin, became dualistic when it pitted the good god Osiris (Oussir) against his bad brother Seth (Oussit), both supposed to be the sons of Ptah, the supreme God. But these gods themselves had a birth. It is from the primordial Ocean Noum or Noun that Atum or Aten, the Sun God, was born, from whom was born in turn a first divine couple, Chou and Tefnut. It was tears of joy that Atum shed during this fatherhood that men would be born. Chou and Tefnut gave birth to Ghêb, the Earth, and to Nut, the Sky, which gave birth to Isis, Osiris and Nephthys. The birth of Osiris had also taken place in Amentêt (or Amenti), the residence of the blessed, located in the West (this is undoubtedly Atlantis), where Nut, still a virgin, had been fertilized by the Spirit, the latter having taken the form of an ibis. It was only later, under the influence of Semitic invaders, who notably revered Seth, the third son of Adam and Eve, that the Egyptians added Seth to the children that Nut would have fathered. And it is after the departure of these invaders from Egypt that Seth (Typhon) will be made the evil spirit, the evil brother of Osiris as told in the myth of Osiris.

The Osirian religion being a mystery cult, one had to be initiated into it. Abraham and Melkitsedek were probably, and also Moses, who transmitted this initiation to Joshua. There would therefore be a Gnostic tradition among the Hebrews, which would be transmitted alongside the official monolaster doctrine, a tradition where Osiris became Adam, of whom Seth is not, however, the bad brother, but on the contrary a son, destined to replace Abel, killed by Cain the reprobate. One of the essential elements of the Osirian esoteric doctrine is the principle of emanations: there is only one God, luminous and perfect, but He can make emanate from Him beings who participate in Him while having a personality distinct from Him. hers. Hence the apparent polytheism of the Egyptian religion. Hence also the aeons and angels of many Gnostic doctrines, and even the Christian Trinity, which would be a variant of the Egyptian trinity and the Hindu Trimurti. It was against the excesses of this conception and its consequences that the pharaoh Amenhotep IV reacted, who changed his name to Akehnaton and wanted to reestablish a more refined monotheism. But, after his death, official polytheism will regain the upper hand, and this is why some hypothesize that Moses will lead almost all the Hebrews out of Egypt, followed also by a few initiated Egyptians and even by a few foreigners. The Osirian religion having evolved in Egypt, it gave birth, in the Hellenistic era, to the Hermetic doctrine, named after Hermes, the Greek god to whom Thoth, the ancient Egyptian legislator, would be assimilated.

By visiting their tombs in Osirian form, the Egyptians were showing that they had found their Higher Self within – what we would today call their "Buddha Consciousness" or "Christ Consciousness."

The myth of Dionysus

Dionysus is the only Greek god born to a mortal mother. From Homer and Hesiod, he is presented as the son of Zeus and Semele, daughter of the king of Thebes Cadmus and Harmony. Semele, pushed by Hera, jealous, disguised as her nurse, asks to contemplate Zeus, with whom she is pregnant, in all his majesty. Zeus, having promised, must present himself with his lightning which kills Semele on the spot. Zeus then takes his son from his mother's womb and, cutting his thigh, sews the child there to bring his gestation to term. This is the origin of the expression "to be born from the thigh of Jupiter", the thigh being a euphemistic designation for the sexual organs, Dionysus could then be considered to have come directly from the sperm of Zeus.

In another version, the Orphic version of the myth, Dionysus-Zagreus is the son of Persephone and Zeus. Hera, jealous, asks the titans (Cronos, Ocean, Iapetus, etc.) to get rid of the newborn. The giants lure the child Dionysus-Zagreus with toys (which will remain mystical: the spinning top, the bullnose, the knucklebones and the mirror), massacre him and cut him into pieces which they cook in a cauldron and consume . Athena, however, picks up her heart in a chest and gives it to Zeus by means of which he then impregnates Semele. Dionysus is then resurrected. It is to this second tradition, where he is the son of Zeus and Persephone, that the myth of the dismemberment of Dionysus is linked.

For a more specific narration on *the Mysteries of Dionysus – The Quest for Mystical Ecstasy* , watch Ludovic Richer tell us about it [72].

Unlike Osiris who resurrects in the land of the dead, from the unconscious , Dionysus dies the first time , also dismembered , in this case by the Titans shortly after his birth , but he was reborn on earth in Greece among the living. Continue with the text by Marie-Laure Colonna *Dionysos or time regained* [73].

The Dionysia were festivals marking the equinoxes. Mystery cults were not bacchanalian ceremonies.

Whatever the version, Dionysus experiences two births, which explains one of his epithets "the twice-born".

There is a tradition to say that Greek tragedy, in its oldest form, had no other object than the sufferings of Dionysus. For Nietzsche, in his book *The Birth of Tragedy,* art is at the same time what makes the horror of becoming bearable: " *It*

---

[72]Video Ludovic Richer: <tinyurl.com/culte-Dionysos>.
[73]< academia.edu/63000368 >.

alone is able to bend this disgust for the horror and the absurdity of existence to be transformed into representations capable of making life possible ."

By his death and resurrection, his worship rendered with bread and wine, Dionysus, would be a pagan antecedent of the story of Jesus [74].

The Myth of Eternal Return

According to Mircea Eliade, historian of religions, the universe is subject to the law of eternal beginnings. World history unfolds cyclically. Babylonian astronomers had discovered that the revolutions of the planets, the annual revolutions of the sun and the moon are subsets of the same common period, the great year, at the end of which the sun, the moon and the planets resume their initial position relative to the fixed stars. They concluded that the life of the universe goes through the same phases eternally.

The notion of cycle will then permeate numerous myths which were inspired by astronomy and the movement of the stars. The distinction between the past and the future is erased to give way to a more global vision of time, a vision of the eternal return anticipated by these ancient and contemporary peoples.

In all societies, there is a conception of the end and the beginning of a temporal period, based on biological rhythms and the regeneration of life. Man needs to set benchmarks in the flow of time. Thus, every new year is a resumption of time at its beginning, reproducing the creation of the world, the return to primordial unity, the passage from chaos to

---

[74] G. Mackey explored the Mysteries in his work *The Symbolism of Freemasonry* or listen (in English) <tinyurl.com/Dionysos-et-Jesus>. For an interpretation of the *Pieced Body of Dionysus* by Frédérique Ildefonse: <tinyurl.com/corps-morcele>.

order. The past ceases to be irreparable, what has been can be relived and the world can be re-enchanted. This concept is present in ancient Egypt, in the mystery rites of the ancient Greeks, in India and the Far East, in Celtic traditions and in pre-Columbian America.

The general idea of cyclical time probably first appeared in Hindu thought. Samsara, the flow, designates the transmigration of souls, the cycle of rebirths, the main driving force of which is karma. Men are then destined to be perpetually reborn until they reach awakening, enlightenment. In this conception of life, death is only a simple passage from one existence to another.

The doctrine of the transmigration of souls was closely associated with the Orphics, and with the followers of the philosopher and mathematician Pythagoras. According to his teachings, the soul, barely leaving the body, finds itself in prison in another body. She is condemned to constantly reincarnate because of a primitive taint. The cycle of reincarnations is endless for those who are not initiated.

In ancient Egypt, the myth of eternal return is that of the solar disk, the floods of the Nile, the days and the seasons. Even beyond death, we find this myth, because there is a cosmic unity; the law of Thoth reported by the texts of the sarcophagi begins as follows: "Everything is cycle. I start to live again after my death. I am resurrected after death."

Even today, numerous agrarian rites, mimicking this renaissance, continue in Europe. The whole doctrine is present in Nietzsche's *Thus Spoke Zarathustra* : "All things return eternally, and we ourselves with them. Everything goes away, everything comes back; the wheel of being rolls eternally. Everything dies and everything blooms again, the year of being unfolds eternally."

The philosophical and metaphysical question that arises behind it is, on the one hand, that of cyclical time, indefinite, unthinkable at its end and therefore structured in a circularity which goes from a creation to an ultimate chaos, where everything recasts. and is refound represented by a circle, on the other hand, that of a theology, of a terminal finality, represented by a linear progression. The entry into a historicized time is inaugurated first by the transgression of Adam and Eve, then by the exit from Egypt. At the same time, the representation of cosmic time is maintained thanks to the importance given to calendar cycles and rituals (shabbat, fallow, jubilee). It is with the Bible that the idea of a time which unfolds from a beginning and which moves towards an end is born. Christian theology, from the first councils, attempted to promote a linearity which it opposed to the cyclical representations of so-called "pagan" civilizations, ruining cyclical agricultural representations and establishing a single historical time. For Papus, the apprentice will then be the seed that blooms; the companion. the plant that flowers; the master, the plant which bears fruit and the fruit which falls to generate new plants through the fruiting which releases the seeds contained within it.

The eternal return, also, is not exactly a return to "the same." In the labyrinth, the dialectic of "same" and "other" fades. The labyrinthine journey is a regressive progression: the spiral forces every "traveler" to retrace their steps, so we only approach the center by moving away from it. We move forward with memory. Leaving the labyrinth, returning to the light, does not mean finding a previous state which is the same – which is indicated by repetition – it is a new birth. We can speak of a "forward regression" to the extent that memory, Ariadne's thread, announces a future. It is an eschatological memory, a memory of hope [75].

---

[75] Philippe Borgeaud, Exercise in mythology , page 36.

We can say that cyclical time is an external time (chronos) measuring the time of clocks within which an irreversible linear time (Kairos) of individual life is experienced. "Chronos highlights the *quantitative* , calculable and repetitive element of the temporal process" ; "Kairos on the contrary designates a *qualitative element* which is distinguished by its absolute singularity".

THE Solar myths

A symbolic story is a story combined in such a way that the evolution of the characters accurately indicates the evolution of nature. Modern mythologists have shown that all the stories relating to Hindu, Egyptian, Greek, Roman deities and even Christ were only more or less perfect paintings of the movement of the sun; hence the name "solar myths given " to all these stories.

In most solar myths or legends, there is a hero struck to death by a monster, a genius, an assassin. This hero has a wife, a son. He is the sun, his wife is the earth, his son is man. Despite their differences in narrative, these myths all achieve the same end: sometimes the hero is resurrected, sometimes he is avenged and replaced by his son. The Freemason, as the widow's son, is the child who becomes a man by taking Hiram's place.

With the opening and closing times of the outfits, the presence of the two luminaries, the starry sky, the words of the ritual concerning the Venerable placed in the east to open the works, the candlestick with seven branches, Freemasonry is well positioned at the heart of solar allegories. The lodge is oriented according to the solar course and the Johannine festivals are linked to solar worship.

Dressed in the third grade, those who move inside the temple no longer mark the angles as they did in the previous grade, in the image of the path of the sun but also in the image of earthly life which rushes in a single impulse from birth to death. The assassination of Hiram, taken in the figurative or allegorical style, is like the passion of Osiris, like that of Adonis, Atys, and Mithra, a fact of the imagination of astronomer priests, who had for purpose the painting of the absence of the sun on the earth.

The myth of Innana/Ishtar

Ancient Sumerian texts describe several deities, both male and female, but one goddess was worshiped above all other deities for thousands of years. This is Inanna, the Great Astral Goddess worshiped since the beginning of Sumerian culture. She transformed into Ishtar later in Akkadian Mesopotamia, into Anat and Atargatis in ancient Syria, into Ashtoreth and Astarte in Canaan and Israel, into Aphrodite in Cyprus, into Athena and Aphrodite in Greece. Married to Tammouz (see the following myth below), lover rejected by Gilgamesh on whom she will take revenge.

An ancient poem from Nipur, a cultural and spiritual center of Akkadia, relates the story of Inanna's descent into the world below. In the midst of her reign as Queen of Heaven and Earth, Inanna decides to descend to the Underworld, the realm of death ruled by her dark sister, Ereshkigal. Foresighted, she instructs her minister, the goddess Ninshubar, to wait for her return in three days. If after three days she still had not returned, Ninshubar would lament and beat the drum for her. Inanna must pass through seven portals on her descent. At each portal, she is forced to abandon elements of construction of her cultural and social identity (her 7 magical powers stolen from the god Enki (which means who am I?), fundamental to life). When she finally reaches the final cavernous chamber where Ereshkigal is located, she is completely naked and lowered.

The seven gates through which Inanna passes and descends into the Lower World recall the seven levels of the ziggurat, like the seven chakras of the Hindu psychic body, and represent the seven levels of consciousness. Inanna must descend from the highest level of her divinity to the most primitive state of consciousness.

Ereshkigal and the seven judges of the World Below surround the helpless goddess and pass judgment against her. Because she has passed through the realm of the dead, she too must die. She is killed and her corpse is hung on a meat hook. After three days and three nights, Ninshubar begins to wail, beating his drum, complaining to the gods so that Inanna will return. Enki, the god of water and wisdom, sends two asexual spirits who free Inanna by giving her food and the water of life. When Inanna is resurrected, she can return home, but on one condition: she must find someone to replace her in the Underworld.

Its rebirth prefigures in the resurrection rites of the mystery cults which flourished in the classical world and in which the initiates received their new life thanks to the body and blood of a divinity. This concept is symbolically taken up in Christian communion rites.

The myth of Tammuz

Tammuz or Tammuz, Dumuzi among the Sumerians, is the god of vegetation, symbol of the death and rebirth of nature.

Every year during the autumn he dies, dragged towards the underworld by the seven Gallus demons. Then, drought and desolation reign on earth. But Ishtar his wife will go and look for him there.

Ishtar, goddess of love and war, who governs life and death, married the shepherd Tammouz who thus became the sovereign of the city. One day, Ishtar (Innana) decides to go down to Hell, the abode of the dead, to supplant her older sister, to abolish death there. She succeeds in entering her sister's palace, but must strip herself of all her clothes and give up all her power. Her sister then stares at her with the gaze of death and her body becomes inert. Messengers from the world above manage to reach her, but the seven judges of hell hold her back, saying: "Who then, having descended into hell, has ever returned from hell without harm ? If Ishtar wants to come back from the underworld, let her provide a replacement. The replacement will be her husband Tammouz. Faced with the lamentations of Tammouz, the sovereign of the underworld, regretting the loss of her husband, obtains from the gods authorization for her cyclical return among the living to restore life to its fertile power; only half of the year in the world of the dead and his sister will replace him for the other half.

When agriculture and breeding were established facts, and as the role of the male in generation appeared as a vital element, we added to the *Genitrix* , that she was called Mother Earth or queen of the skies or otherwise , a husband destined to play the essential role of procreator, even if in Mesopotamia, he was only the servant or son of the Goddess, producer of all life. In agricultural communities such as those of the Tigris and Euphrates valleys, when the cult of birth was linked to the seasonal cycle and the rites of vegetation, the Earth Goddess was considered to hold the fertility of the entire nature and thus became responsible for the periodic renewal of the soil, renewal which occurred after the cold of winter or the drought of summer. As a result, she took the form of a goddess with multiple aspects, with a maternal character of which Ishtar is only one of the names.

Allegorical necessity demanded the union of the goddess who embodied fertility in general with the god who personified the creative power of spring. According to the normal cycle of the seasons, he died and passed into the abode of night and death, from which ordinary mortals cannot return. In Mesopotamia, mother earth was the inexhaustible source of new life. It was she who allowed the vegetation to renew itself, who watched over the harvests and who presided over the propagation of the human race as well as that of animal species. Under her aspect of Inanna-Ishtar, through her marriage with Doummouzi-Tammouz, god who embodied spring renewal, she symbolized and even effectively produced the renewal of vegetation, which freed the earth from harmful sterility. But this union only became effective after the perpetually renewed struggle between the two opposing natural forces : that of fertility and that of sterility. Once this struggle was victoriously ended by the triumph of good, Tammouz saved from the kingdom of death and restored to the light in all the blossoming of his virility, life spread again on the earth. It was on the return of the "resurrected child" of the Goddess that the new impetus which made the vital flow spring forth from the parched earth depended.

This myth made it possible to explain to humans the succession of seasons and the different modifications of nature during the course of the year; in autumn and winter, Tammouz is absent among the living, on his return in spring and in summer, life reappears on earth. After his death and resurrection, he will be placed among the gods. His cult spread in Syria, Phoenicia and as far as Judea, and he then also bore the names of Adonis, Eshmoûn, Simon, Doumouzi.

The myth of Adonis

Adonis is the hero type of all initiations. Greek women made it a pious duty to cry at ceremonies commemorating the death of Adonis, killed by a furious boar. This legend illustrates the solar rite where the sun first fertilizes nature during spring and summer. After this period, this star loses its productive faculties. This is why, in the autumn, Adonis, going hunting, is struck down by a wild boar (symbol of winter), which mutilates him and deprives him of his generative faculties. Before being returned to Venus, who deplores his loss, this god, whose mutilation and death are only a fiction, must spend the other six months of the year with the Venus (or nature) of the lower hemisphere, this woman of the constellations, placed on the spheres, in front of the serpent, *præ serpens* , from which the name Proserpina comes. So here is the sun of spring or summer, dying in autumn, only to return the following spring.

The myth of Persephone/Proserpina

Persephone occupies an important place in the cults of many cities, particularly those of Eleusis, Thebes and Megara, as well as in Sicily and Arcadia.

An infernal divinity, she is also originally a wheat goddess, like her mother Demeter. Among the Greeks, soil fertility was closely linked to death, and seed grains were kept in the dark during the summer months for germination, before sowing in the fall. This return of life after burial is symbolized by the myth of Persephone, kidnapped, then returned, which gave birth to the rites of the Eleusinian mysteries. For the faithful, the return to earth of the goddess is a formal promise of their own resurrection. This myth of agriculture can be compared to the myth of Mithras.

The breakdown of a natural and close relationship between Persephone and her mother, the harvest goddess Demeter, is an opportunity to reflect on an issue central to any process of emergence: the confrontation with estrangement. The kidnapping of the young girl by her uncle, the king of the dead, the refusal of the Korê (the young girl) to unite with him, the compromise found between the will of Hades and the incessant resistance of the mother and of the girl facing the cut, lead to a questioning about the work of the negative, more precisely about the tension between necessary separation and impossible separation and about the meaning of this tension for the creative process.

The myth of Demeter-Ceres

This goddess is in fact a single divinity honored by the entire universe, but in different forms, under different names, through different ceremonies. The Phrygians, the first born of men, call her the Pessinontian mother of the Gods; the Athenians, Cecropian Minerva; the Cyprians, Paphian Venus; the Cretans, Diana Dictynne; the Sicilians, Proserpina Scygian; the Eleusinians, the ancient Goddess Ceres; she is nicknamed Cabiria by the Thebans; by others, Juno; by still others, Bellona; some, Hecate; and some others, Rhamnusia. But the Egyptians, who are instructed in the ancient doctrine, honor her with ceremonies proper to her and call her by her true name, Queen Isis. Demeter, whose name, probably a concatenation of the Greek words meaning "earth and mother", was the goddess of agriculture and the harvest. She represented the cultivated and fertile earth unlike other goddesses like Gaia or Rhea who personified the earth as matter. It is she who facilitates the germination and growth of plants.

Daughter of Kronos and Rhea, she is one of the twelve Olympians even if she preferred to reside in Eleusis in contact with the earth rather than on Olympus.

She was assimilated by the Romans under the name of Ceres which was a very ancient Latin divinity associated with the harvest. Formerly in Attica, the dead were called cereal people.

When Hades, ruler of the dead, kidnapped his daughter Persephone to make her his wife, Demeter went in search of her and neglected the crops of the earth. Taking the form of an old woman named *Doso* , she wandered for nine (9) days. Realizing that a famine threatened mortals, Zeus decided to send Hermes to the kingdom of Hades to ask him to return Persephone to her mother. But Persephone had eaten six seeds of the pomegranate offered by Hades, as a last ruse to keep it with him; tradition dictated that anyone who ate in the realm of the dead could not leave it. Zeus agreed that Persephone would spend the six months cultivating on the land with her mother and the six months of the rest of the year with her husband. It is from this myth of Persephone that the cycle of the seasons in Greek mythology was born.

His worship is based on the rhythm of the seasons; it is the source of the Eleusinian Mysteries. The secret of his Mysteries was very well guarded and its disclosure was punishable by the death penalty; Aeschylus was almost condemned.

Demeter was also particularly venerated by women, for example during the Thesmophoria in Athens, a ceremony which received its name from the epithet of the goddess *Thesmophoros* (the Lawgiver) and which was reserved for women; they worshiped fertility both for themselves and for the city; Aristophanes makes them the subject of his comedy, *The Thesmophoria* .

Temples of Demeter, called *megara* , were often found in forests.

Bernard Dov Hercenberg remarks , in his article *The myth of Demeter and the tension between attempted separation and impossible separation* , that the movement of return which is present in the myth of Demeter is reminiscent of certain parameters of the Hegelian *Aufhebung* and Nietzschean *Überwindung* . Not only because this eternal return implies a confrontation with the negative but because these comings and goings are done through movements of ascent and descent. Because Persephone is the one who repeatedly sinks into the heart of the earth to go to the kingdom of Hades and repeatedly comes back into the open sky to find her mother. Persephone's movement to face negativity is accomplished by incessant rises and falls which, in short, circle around negativity on the one hand, and life and light on the other. These descents and these ascents allow a recognition of differences and a taking into account of the whole. They articulate a knowledge of which one of the characteristics is, in a certain way, an "overcoming" of the negative and of difference. In this sense, they are reminiscent of the rises and falls that philosophy has spoken about since Plato regarding the relationship between the sensible and the supersensible. The Shinto myth of the goddess Amaterasu is similar to that of Demeter. This feminine divinity is said to have introduced rice cultivation, wheat cultivation and silkworms. In the most famous legend about her, she locks herself in a cave, causing disasters on earth and in the skies.

The **Myth of Mithras**

Mithras is an Indo-European deity. Several Hittite documents confirm its existence from the 2nd millennium BC.

The name Mithra is formed from the Persian *mithri* or *mether* which means Lord, a title given to the god Mithra by a number of inscriptions, in particular Julian the apostate who called him sometimes king of all things, sometimes lord, here witness, there father and sometimes protective. The Gauls had the same idea as the Persians and the Romans, they called the sun Lord of the Roman Empire.

In the absence of texts on Mithraism, written by the followers themselves, the main sources of usable information are the sacred images found in the *mithraea.*

Mithra was born from a fertile rock, the *Petra generatrix* , at the foot of a sacred tree, near a cultic spring, with a Phrygian cap on her head, a hunting knife in one hand and a torch in the other. Shepherds, who came to worship the child god, took care of him and offered him livestock and fruits of the earth. Being naked, he cuts the leaves of a fig tree and makes a loincloth from them, picks the fruits and eats them. Then he sets out to confront the powers that populate the universe.

He meets the primordial bull which was grazing in the mountains, decides to ride it but, in the wild gallop of the beast, Mithra falls and clings to the animal's horns. The exhausted beast, Mithra ties it and loads it on his shoulders. This journey with the bull is called *Transitus*.

When Mithras arrives in the cave, a raven sent by the Sun tells him that he should make a sacrifice. Flanked by two dadophores (who carry torches), Cautès with raised torch and Cautopatès with lowered torch, representing respectively the rising and setting of the sun (or the signs of the zodiac which mark the entry, the first in the hot season, the second in the cold season) one knee on the bull, Mithra plants a knife in its throat turning his eyes towards the raven, messenger of the Sun. Hit in the heart, the bull collapses. From the spine of the bull comes wheat, and from its blood flows wine.

To delve deeper into the origins of the myth, complete with the text by René P. Bacqué de Balagué, *Mithra, a Freemason god, really?*[76]

Furious, the evil spirit Angra Mayniu is unleashed against the benefits of the bull which he decides to annihilate, by sending impure animals to destroy the source of life. Then arrive the dog which eats the grain, the scorpion which squeezes the testicles of the beast with its pincers, the snake drinking the blood from the wound. But the Moon, faithful companion of the Sun, with his help, gathers and purifies the semen of the bull to complete the work of Mithras, giving birth to all kinds of useful animals. Furious, Angra

---

[76]René P. Bacqué de Balagué: <tinyurl.com/Mithra-dieu-franc-macon>.

Mayniu dispatches a multitude of calamities against men, including a flood intended to wipe out humanity from creation. Fortunately Mithras watched and warned a man who built a strong ark to save earthly creations.

Short of imagination, the evil spirit Angra Mayniu temporarily ceases all attempts against men.

After having accomplished the mission that the god Ahura Mazda had entrusted to him, Mithra participates, with his old friend the Sun, in a last solemn banquet, where he eats the bread and drinks the wine. Then he rises to heaven where he will continue to live watching over men and protecting them from evil.

As for the sacrificed bull, it was raised to the sky where it became a constellation.

The myth of Mithras is reminiscent of elements from other traditions. As it predates them, we can ask ourselves the question of the influence of this myth on those of the flood, the solstice, the eucharist, the Ascension, of Jesus in short, and why not of Freemasonry.

The myth of Odin

Odin is the main god of Norse mythology. His role, as with most Norse gods, is complex, given his multiple functions: god of knowledge, victory and death. To a lesser extent, he is also considered the patron of magic, poetry, prophecies, war and hunting.

Odin is depicted as an elderly, bearded, one-eyed man. He is a polymorphic deity. He rides on an eight-legged horse named Sleipnir, armed with his spear Gungnir. When he is in his palace, Valhöll, the two ravens Hugin (thought) and Munin (memory) tell him in his ear what they have seen of the nine worlds. Additionally, two wolves, Geri and Freki, remain at his feet. His throne, Hlidskjalf, allows him to see everything that exists in the nine worlds. Mimir is a giant, the incarnation of memory in Germanic mythology. "Odin wanted to know the runes and reveal them. The runes, these mysterious signs, secret and magical writing, symbols of forbidden knowledge to which the gods had no access. Nine days and nine nights he meditated in the protective shadow of Ygdrasil. Then he asked the other gods to fulfill his desire. It was a real sacrilege to claim this forbidden power from the gods, so they refused. Then Odin requested the arbitration of the Nomes (Celto-Druidic virgin goddesses : **Urd:** the elder sister, winds the threads around the spindle, thus giving life by literally "creating" new destinies. **Verdandi** : spins the wool and chooses the direction that each thread of destiny will take. **Skuld** : the youngest is associated with death which she decides by cutting the threads), the weavers who weave destiny, symbolized by the triskele. The guardians of the dark gates, upon reflection, were favorable to him, but they imposed terrible conditions on him. Odin accepted the sacrifice, with full knowledge of the facts. He leaned over Mimir's fountain. As he saw nothing, he sacrificed his right eye, which fell into the sacred spring. So he lives. He experiences infinite times, the depth of memory, the past and the future of men. Then he pierced his side with his spear and the gods hung him, head down, by one foot, on the sacred yew where he was born. All the buds on the tree began to bleed. For nine terrible nights of suffering, the one-eyed god hung in Ygdrasil. Nine nights, as it takes nine months to make a man... As darkness gave way to the sun, the god was illuminated by the light of the runes finally revealed. Upon discovering the runes, Odin became "the prince of engraved power." Odin taught that runes should be used in all circumstances of life, because they are a guide, a help, they are the hope of the desperate, the faithful companions of the heart broken by loneliness. He was an Aesir god of wisdom and one of the two deities sent in exchange for peace to the Vanir. But the latter, realizing that they had been fooled, beheaded the God and sent his head to the Aesir. However, Odin coated it with a mixture of herbs so that it would not rot and he enchanted it with spells. Once brought back to life, the head was capable of speaking and revealing occult secrets, many truths that no one else knows. Odin placed it under the roots of Yggdrasil near the well with the same name as the mummified head. He thus becomes the guardian of the *Mimisbrunn* , the "source of Mimir", a source which contains wisdom and intelligence.

Mythological ash from primitive Scandinavian religion dating from 2500 BC. Yggdrasil, the world tree comes from the death of Ymir, the primordial giant born from chaos. Killed by his sons, he transformed himself. The giant's blood changed into the sea, his skull was transformed into a rainbow (the Bifrost), his lungs into clouds, his bones into mountains and his hair into a tree-pillar of the world and all natures. Ymir's upheavals created a New World and her rebirth in death. He lives in the world of which he is the only source.

On him rest nine kingdoms. It would have three roots, one of which draws from the fountain of Urd, where the Aesir held council and where the Norns, very wise old witches and feared by the gods, set the length of men's lives, pouring over the tree water from this fountain in order to ensure perpetual sap and greenery. The second root extends towards the land of the giants ; it draws from the fountain of Mimir believed to contain the source of all wisdom; the fountain is guarded by a giant and shelters the head of the god Mimir who holds the secrets of the universe. As for the third root, it comes from Nieflein, the Scandinavian hell, where it is constantly gnawed by a dragon, Nídhögg, but where it constantly regenerates.

In other words, we could say that the world tree draws its energy from lived experiences (ancestral memory), secret knowledge (the secrets of the universe and the gods), and from the destiny of beings (the evolution of consciousness).

On the highest branch of Yggdrasil stands an eagle, while other animals are perched on the other branches: a goat, a deer, from its horns trickles the water which falls into Hvergelmir, a squirrel, Ratatosk, running constantly in the tree, never ceasing to sow discord between the dragon and the eagle.

See the article by Mircea Eliade: *The myth of Yggdrasil, the cosmic tree of the Scandinavians.*[77]

THE Myth of the Cabiri

The Cabiris were gods whose worship was first established on the island of Samothrace, where the Mysteries of Cabiric were practiced. The gods called the Cabiri were originally two, and later four; they are assumed, by Bryant, to refer to Noah and his three sons; the Cabiric Mysteries being a modification of the cult of the moon goddess (Astarteus or Ishtar) to which bows made of acacia wood were dedicated.

In these mysteries there was a ceremony called the "Cabre Death," in which was represented amidst the groans and tears and subsequent rejoicing of the initiates, the death and restoration to life of Cadmillus, the youngest of the Cabiri. Legend has it that he was killed by his three brothers who then fled with his virile parts in a mystical basket. His body, crowned with flowers, was buried at the foot of Mount Olympus. Clement of Alexandria speaks of the legend as the sacred mystery of a brother killed by his brothers or in the original as *frater trucidatus a fratribus* . Some authors assume that the three Cabiri, or Corybantes, symbolize the sun, the moon and the earth, believed to be killed in the eclipse, and cite the words of Hesiod — "Stained with blood and falling into the hands of two celestial bodies ".

------

[77]Mircea Eliade: The myth of Yggdrasil, the cosmic tree of the Scandinavians <tinyurl.com/mythe-d-Yggdrasil>.

The slain Casmillus had the same meaning as the Osirian sun god in Phoenician, Babylonian and Egyptian books. The blood, to which reference is made in the Phrygian version of the Cabiric rites, would recall the cosmogonies with some curious references which can characterize circumcision, the mythical baptism of blood, and the Taurobolium or the baptism of bulls [78].

Goblet D'Aviella recounts in his book *Origin of the grade of master in Freemasonry* (1905): In the mysteries of the Cabires, in Samothrace, the tragic story of the three brothers, Axieros, Axio-kërsos and Axiokersa, was portrayed. . According to the version of the legend reported by Pirmicus Maternus, two of the Cabiri put the third to death and buried him at the foot of Mount Olympus; he was then brought back to life by Hermes. The decoration of certain Etruscan mirrors represents successive scenes from this drama. In one, we see Axieros seized by his brothers, in front of two columns. Corinthian capital. In another, Hermes, accompanied by two satyrs who serve as his acolytes, approaches the body and attempts to resurrect it with his magic wand.

The Cabiric gods were considered the instructors of humanity in all useful knowledge; magical rites, construction, smelting and working of metals, shipbuilding, music, etc., were called Technites or artificers. Sanconiathon says that Ouranos was the father of sculptors, just like Hiram the father or Abiv of masons, metalworkers, sculptors and dyers, and indeed a Cabir.

It is generally supposed that these mysteries were instituted in honor of Atys, the son of Cybele or Demeter, of whom Cadmillus was only another name. According to Macrobius, Atys was one of the names of the sun, and we know that the

---

[78] John Yarker, *The Arcane Schools* , 1909:
<hermetics.org/yarker2.html>.

mysteries were celebrated at the vernal equinox. They lasted three days, during which they represented in the person of Atys, or Cadmillus (the youngest of the Cabiri), the enigmatic death of the sun in winter, and its regeneration in spring. In all probability, in the initiation, the candidate was going through a drama whose subject was violent death. The "cabric death" was, in fact, a legend, as one can understand, very similar in spirit to that of the third degree of Hiramic Freemasonry.

**So is the epopty of Hiram presented to the Freemasons
a tale, a legend or a myth?**
What do you think?

About the Author

Jacques-André editor
TU, Letters of Passion, 2001 (Laure de Noves Prize)

EDITIONS of La Hutte
To light the way, A philosophical approach to Freemasonry , 2011
Vocabulary of the Apprentice Freemason , 2nd ^{edition} , 2012
Vocabulary of the Freemason Companion , 2012
Master Freemason Vocabulary , 2013
Drawing elements with ruler and compass, The Masonic Concordance , 2015
What does it mean to cut your stone ?, 2015

EDITIONS ledifice.net
Gathering what is scattered , 2020
Vocabulary of the Apprentice Freemason , 3rd ^{edition} , 2020
Vocabulary of the Freemason Companion , 2nd ^{edition} , 2021

Ubik EDITIONS
Once upon a time, Hiram , 2021
Masonic gestures , 2021

Numérilivre EDITIONS _
Masonic traces, the spirit of geometry , 2022

Dervy EDITIONS
Vagabond Dictionary of Masonic Thought , 2017 (**literary prize of the Masonic Institute of France** , Essays and Symbolism category)
Freemason. How to move from profane to sacred , 2023

www.ingramcontent.com/pod-product-compliance
Lightning Source LLC
Chambersburg PA
CBHW012304240726
48656CB00008B/2543